PRIMARY MEDIA EDUCATION

A CURRICULUM STATEMENT

BFI NATIONAL WORKING PARTY
FOR PRIMARY MEDIA EDUCATION

edited by

Cary Bazalgette

BFI Education Department
21 Stephen Street
London W1P 1PL

January 1989

Production: Rachael Stroud (Design, graphics and word processing)
                     Jim Adams (Photography)
                     Underhill (Plymouth) Limited (Printing)

Acknowledgements: this booklet is the outcome of many people's work. For a full list of acknowledgements, see p. 98

Reprinted 1989, 1991

British Library Cataloguing in Publication Data

BFI National Working Party for Primary Media Education
Primary Media Education: A Curriculum Statement

1. Great Britain. Primary Schools. Curriculum Subjects. Media Studies
I. Title II. Bazalgette, Cary III. British Film Institute, Education Department
372.8

ISBN 0-85170-247-3

CONTENTS

Photo: Mike Hamon, Stottesdon School, Shropshire

1 | INTRODUCTION

The curriculum statement which follows is the result of three years' work by the BFI National Working Party for primary media education. The twenty members of this group include classroom teachers, advisers and teacher trainers, with HMI as observers, who have all been engaged in small-scale, informal action research into what good primary media education might look like. The working party was convened and administered by the British Film Institute's Education Department, with a grant from the Calouste Gulbenkian Foundation. With the passing of the 1988 Education Reform Act and preparations for the National Curriculum, the working party feels that it is essential to make a contribution to these developments and argue for a place for media education within the new curriculum.

Primary media education is still relatively new. The main impetus to its development came from the DES Report, *Popular TV and Schoolchildren,* in April 1983, which stated that "specialist courses in media studies are not enough: all teachers should be involved in examining and discussing television programmes with young people" (p.27). Over the ensuing five years, media teachers and others have extended this principle to all the media and called for education about the media to be seen as an entitlement of all children, from nursery school onwards. The practical realisation of this idea in actual classrooms is, naturally, taking a little longer, and the working party was formed to ensure that such work was described, shared and criticised constructively.

Through our termly seminars and four sets of working papers, we have developed accounts of practice and explored the principles informing that practice. In the past year, we have begun to develop an account of the key areas of knowledge and understanding that, in our view, form the basis of media education. Upon these we have built this curriculum statement.

The statement should be regarded more as a discussion document than a definitive account of media education in the primary school. Such an account must wait until further research and curriculum development is undertaken; we are currently seeking funding for a National Media Education Project which will contribute to that process. In the meantime this statement, with its gaps and uncertainties, may serve as a basis for further work. We hope to receive constructive comment and ideas for its development.

This booklet has been sent free of charge to media advisers in Britain and abroad, to National Curriculum Subject Working Parties, the Department of Education and Science, and the National Curriculum Council. Further copies are available from BFI Publications, 29 Rathbone Street, London W1P 1AG, at a nominal charge.

BFI Education has now published *Secondary Media Education: A Curriculum Statement*, which is also available from BFI Publications.

Cary Bazalgette
Convenor of the Primary Working Party
British Film Institute Education Department
April 1991

2 OUR VIEW OF MEDIA EDUCATION

Why a Curriculum Statement?

As our most significant sources of shared information, education and entertainment, the media deserve more informed and critical attention than they currently get. Such attention should be developed in schools, as well as in public discourse.

There is, however, a need for clear statements about what kind of media education is appropriate; what its conceptual basis is; what constitutes good classroom practice; where it should be located in the curriculum; what the difference is between media education and media studies. The English Working Party for the National Curriculum has commented favourably on media education, as follows:

> We have considered media studies largely as part of the exploration of contemporary culture, alongside more traditional literary texts. Television and film and video form substantial elements of children's experience out of school which teachers must take into account. Our assumption is that children should have the opportunity to apply their critical faculties to these major parts of contemporary culture.
>
> Both drama and media studies deal with fundamental questions of language, interpretation and meaning. These seem to us so central to the traditional aims and concerns of English teaching that we would strongly recommend that programmes of study in English should include exploration of both areas. We recognise, however, that drama and media studies also have their own academic integrity: in the secondary school they may exist separately elsewhere on the timetable as specialist subjects outside the National Curriculum. We believe that the English curriculum should prepare children for possible later study of these subjects as separate options. We would wish to stress, however, that we do not see inclusion of drama and media studies activity within English programmes of study as in any way a replacement for specialist study.
>
> *(English for Ages 5 to 11, 14.3 and 14.4, p.61)*

The rest of the report has little to say about media education, reflecting the continuing uncertainty about exactly how media education *would* be included in programmes of study and, as stated in 14.11, "embodied within the three profile components". The curriculum statement which is contained in the following sections of this booklet includes a response to *English for Ages 5 to 11,* but it also goes well beyond that in describing separate areas of knowledge and understanding, attainment targets, profile components and curriculum locations of media education as an endeavour which has its own integrity as well as being genuinely cross-curricular. It also provides a comprehensive and detailed account of just what media education is.

Our View of Media Education

Media education in the primary school seeks to increase children's critical understanding of the media - namely, television, film, video, radio, photography, popular music, printed materials, and computer software. How they work, how they produce meanings, how they are organised and how audiences make sense of them, are the issues that media education addresses.

Primary media education aims to develop systematically children's critical and creative powers through analysis and production of media artefacts. This also deepens their understanding of the pleasure and entertainment provided by the media. Media education aims to create more active and critical media users who will demand, and could contribute to, a greater range and diversity of media products.

Media education is primarily associated with the "new" media of television, film and radio, but the range of practices described in this curriculum statement clearly has relevance to all public media of expression and communication, including books. True literacy in our time encompasses media education.

Media studies is the term now generally used to describe specialist media education courses, whether as separate examinable subjects in the upper secondary school and in further and higher education, or as specific modules or components within other subject areas or vocational training. Media studies courses have been established for some time now: there are five GCSE syllabi, which were taken by more than 10,000 students in 1988. A recent study undertaken by the National Foundation for Educational Research and the British Film Institute suggests that perhaps 35% of secondary schools now undertake some form of media studies, many of them throughout the secondary age range. New media studies courses and course components are proliferating in higher education and attracting large numbers of students. The media industries themselves are a growing sector of the economy. It can thus be argued that media education in the primary and lower secondary phases will feed an established and growing area of study and of work opportunities.

Kamer Bashir and Halima Begum, Kettlebridge Nursery First School, Sheffield, playing with a camera and pretending to take a picture. Photo: Sue Van Noort

3 | EXPLANATION OF TERMS

In this Curriculum Statement we have made every effort to avoid using the specialist language employed in some advanced media studies courses. However, there are still some terms that we feel are useful but that may seem off-putting at first: not necessarily because the words themselves are difficult, but because we use them in an unusual way. Some of these, like text and agency, are ones we feel we have to resort to in order to convey the breadth of media education's concerns. Others are more specific technical terms. We have printed in bold italics the words that we think may cause difficulties, the first time each one appears, and we list them below, with brief explanations.

agency   we needed a term that was broader than "author" or "producer" but could include these, in order to convey the variety of ways, many of them collective or *institutional*, in which media *texts* (see below) get made. This term was taken from media education curriculum guidelines being prepared in Australia.

audience   by which we mean *any* recipients of a media text, whether readers of a book (who are usually alone) or people watching a film (who are usually all together in a cinema).

code   what results when *conventions* are systematically organised so that the members of the group who know the code can be relied upon to interpret it in a particular way. So "everyone" can recognise a news broadcast even if they switch on in the middle.

convention   the elements of a code, or any broadly agreed way of signalling a particular meaning: eg, having mistletoe or snowmen on a Christmas card is a convention.

genre   French word meaning "type", applied to any accepted group of texts, such as detective novels or Western films, that have clearly recognisable features in common. Hence *generic* and *generically*.

institutions   can be used to mean the actual organisations such as the BBC; or more broadly, to indicate a whole set of professional practices and accepted meanings, such as "the institution of television".

media   all the ways that can be used to express and communicate ideas. Often used to refer only to modern "mass" media such as television; our usage is intended to be much broader than that. Note that it is a *plural* noun, hence "the media *are* ..." (not "is").

media forms   we use this term to indicate broad categories of media, such as news, fiction etc.

read   using this term to describe what you do with a film or a radio broadcast (or any other text) is partly to act as a reminder that making sense of any medium is an active process to which we bring our own previous understanding. It's also to avoid using "read/view/listen" every time.

specificity   what it is about something that makes it different from other things; the quality of being specific.

text   a perhaps unsatisfactory way of solving the problem of what word to use when you want to refer to a book and/or a film, a radio or TV programme, a newspaper, a video, etc all at once, which media education often has to do since it argues that the same conceptual approaches can be used with any of them.

Sophie Lee, aged 7, Oundle Primary School, Northants

Technical Terms

Understanding technical terms is not a necessary preliminary to media education, and we have kept these to a minimum. We found it necessary to include the following, particularly in the Attainment Targets section. Most of them are useful ways of identifying aspects of film or video production with which most children will already be familiar.

chromakey   apparatus used in television to insert one image into another one (eg, an illustration behind a newsreader, or "flying" effects).

continuity announcements   the announcements between programmes on television and radio, which tell you what is coming next, what's on the other channel, and so on.

cut   the usual way of changing abruptly from one shot to another; hence *cross-cutting:* changing from one scene to another and back again (eg, to show simultaneous actions). Other ways of changing shots are: fade (image fades away to black); dissolve or mix (new image mingles with old one before replacing it).

dolly   moving the camera along on trolley or rails to follow movement or reveal a setting.

mixing-desk   apparatus in a TV studio by which a director and/or vision mixer can switch from one camera to another, add sound tracks, etc, in the process of recording or broadcasting.

pan   horizontal swivelling of the camera to follow movement or reveal a scene.

scheduling   process of planning the mix and timing of programmes on a particular channel, over the day, the week, and longer.

serial   a continuing narrative divided into episodes, often with "cliffhangers" at the end of each one (eg, *Coronation Street*).

series   a collection of factual or fictional programmes, each of which is complete in itself, but contains similar subject matter, or the same characters and situations, as the others. Some drama series acquire serial characteristics over time (eg, *London's Burning*).

storyboard   part of planning a film, video, or tape-slide: key moments are sketched to show how they should look in the finished product, and explanatory notes or script written beside/underneath. Teachers can give children pre-drawn storyboard formats - a set of blank frames down or across the page - to plan their production.

tape-slide   a set of slides arranged in sequence with accompanying sounds, voices, music etc on tape. Not a poor substitute for video or film, but a satisfying form in its own right. Equipment can be bought to "cue" the tape to the slides and change slides automatically; more than one slide projector can be used, to fade and blend the images.

tilt   swivelling the camera up or down, to follow movement or reveal a scene.

voice-over   the voice of an unseen speaker accompanying images, eg commentary, soliloquy, etc.

wipe   the process by which one shot seems to push or wipe another off the screen: in older films this was done with straight horizontal, vertical or diagonal lines; computer effects in video now mean images can flip, ripple, dwindle to a vanishing point, etc.

zoetrope   drum-shaped optical toy lined with a series of images; when spun, the images appear to move if viewed through vertical slots in the sides.

zoom   alteration of the focal length of the lenses in a film or video camera so that the camera seems to rush towards, or away from, the subject.

4 | KEY AREAS OF KNOWLEDGE AND UNDERSTANDING IN MEDIA EDUCATION

Because media education should, ideally, permeate and underpin much of what is taught in the primary school, it is important to have a clear sense of what it entails. What should media-educated children know, understand and be able to do?

Media education differs from many other types of "school knowledge" in that it depends crucially on the knowledge that children have gained informally outside school: in the home, the peer group and in the world at large. Media education should recognise this knowledge and help children to organise it and articulate it as well as extending and diversifying it. Teaching about the media is thus likely to encourage the kind of relationship between school and home in which the child's experiences outside school ("the programmes I like"; "the photos we took on holiday") have a real significance and need to be built into the learning that goes on in the classroom.

On this basis, the school can offer new experiences and ideas. Children may well have done some photography, sound taping or video making at home, but in school they can undertake these in different circumstances - individually or as part of a peer group - and for different audiences. The experience of collective viewing and discussion in large groups is different from the domestic setting, requires different skills, and helps to build up a concept of *audience*. The school can introduce a greater diversity to the already rich experience most children have of the media. Independent video and film, different genres of photography, or small-scale newspaper and magazine production can alert children to the possibilities of innovation and change.

In order to develop children's practical skills and understanding of the media systematically, teachers need to be conscious of a number of areas of knowledge and understanding which can act as a framework for organising media education. These areas can be signposted by the following questions, which could be asked of any media *text* - and indeed commonly are.

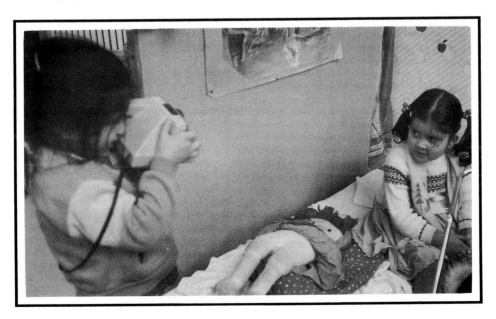

Nursery child at Netley School, London, taking a polaroid photograph of children playing house. Photo: Anne Hawes

SIGNPOST QUESTIONS

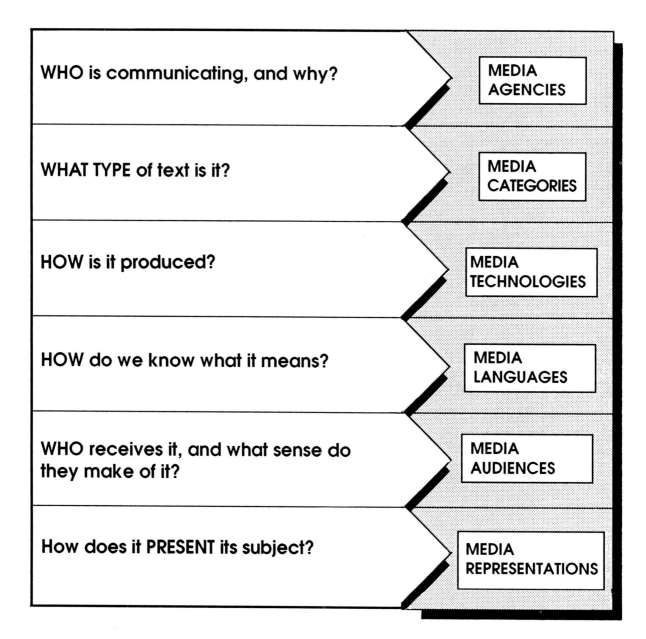

WHO is communicating, and why?	**MEDIA AGENCIES**
WHAT TYPE of text is it?	**MEDIA CATEGORIES**
HOW is it produced?	**MEDIA TECHNOLOGIES**
HOW do we know what it means?	**MEDIA LANGUAGES**
WHO receives it, and what sense do they make of it?	**MEDIA AUDIENCES**
How does it PRESENT its subject?	**MEDIA REPRESENTATIONS**

These questions are all interdependent, so the areas of knowledge and understanding that they indicate cannot be taught separately or in a hierarchy (eg from "easy" to "hard"). At any age level, elements of each area will be considered. For the sake of clarity and detail, we expand upon them separately in the rest of this section.

WHO IS COMMUNICATING, AND WHY?
Media Agencies

Young children often use the word "they" in questions or comments to one another about a media text, as in "I wonder how they made the car crash through the wall", without a clear sense of who "they" are. Older children will ask "I wonder how the film makers made it look like the car crashed through the wall". They have a clearer sense that media texts are produced by someone: a sense of *agency.* At first this is a limited, personal idea: a photograph comes from a photographer; a film is made by people in a studio or perhaps just a camera operator. Later, children can perceive that most photographs we see are not in the same form as our family snapshots, but have been printed and published. Another process has intervened; additional decisions have been made. Media education extends these understandings by providing knowledge about the people and *institutions* who produce media texts. This would include:

- *knowledge gained from their own production processes* about the range of tasks involved in making a text. A group of children making a sound tape on their own will have to work out ways of signalling to each other when to start and stop the tape, who is to give the signal, whether a separate person is needed to take care of the microphone, and so on. So they will be learning:

  - that there are a number of tasks
  - what each task involves
  - what roles the tasks entail for the personnel involved
  - how the roles can relate to another.

- *knowledge gained from other media texts* about who has produced them. Looking at the covers and title pages of books, at the credits of a film or TV programme, at company logos on tapes, is one way of doing this: it establishes that there are many people involved in producing a text, that they can be grouped as members of institutions (eg, MCA Records, the BBC) and that there is a hierarchy of roles and jobs (eg, an editor has higher status than an illustrator).

- *knowledge about media institutions* and how they work is harder to come by, but essential to a full understanding of the media. A class of 7 year olds in a Sussex school were surprised to find the word "flesh" used to designate the colour of a crayon. They corresponded with the manufacturers to explain their objection, and even produced a colour chart of the many "flesh" tints available in their own group, none of which was the same as the crayon. The company appeared to dismiss, or resist, their argument, but in fact the word did not appear in their next catalogue. This exchange broadened the children's experience of dealing with a media institution and of how institutions manage change.

Encouraging and following through these kinds of enquiry helps to motivate the more sophisticated questions that we, as well as older children, could be asking about the media:

- The function they serve for us and society
- How they are paid for
- Their relationship with government and other institutions eg. the unions
- The work of media professsionals.

Further questions could be about who own the media and control various aspects of media production.

A fruitful way into this area can be through considering the differences between professional media forms and children's own productions in terms of:

- Editorial priorities - what you put in and what you leave out
- What resources you have, who controls what you do, where the money comes from
- Circulation - how you reach people.

Contrary to expectations children need not be dispirited by these differences. A group of Nottingham infants realised that a national newspaper would not include their story about a local donkey having a foal, but they also knew it was just that kind of information that made their own newspaper interesting to its intended readership.

Investigating media agencies through thinking about other people's work in parallel with their own, develops children's understanding that texts are always made with a purpose. From this should come the realisation that a text can have many purposes, only some of which may be explicit or even discoverable. An advertisement is made to sell a product, but the form it takes may reflect the advertisers' conscious decision to change, for example, the way they represent women. This links with children's understanding of media languages when they realise that everything in a media text is put there on purpose.

This is not to say that everything in a media text will have its intended result, as we explain in more detail under the heading of media audiences. Considering media agencies must include a consideration of the results of their production - for themselves as well as for others.

The producers may be enriched or improverished by their production; they may gain fame or notoriety; individual careers or corporate images may be enhanced or put at risk. These considerations also figure in producers' motives and intentions, and are of course not always discoverable. Once again, children can infer them from their own production practices. If we sell the class magazine for 10p a copy, will we have any money left over? If we include this photo of the head teacher, will she be cross? How to consider such possibilities, make predictions, and choose the best course of action, are also part of media education.

WHAT TYPE OF TEXT IS IT?
Media Categories

Young children will have varied and possibly inconsistent ways of identifying and differentiating media texts: "cartoon", "programme", "film" may all be applied to the same television output. They will differentiate more firmly between different media, such as television, newspaper, radio, books. Media education extends their ability to identify different media and different types of text, and to group these in ways that contribute to their meaning. If you realise that a film is meant to be a fantasy, it is easier to understand why parts of it seem implausible.

After identifying different media, children should explore their *specificity*. How does a written story change when it's made into a film? Do the same things appear in TV, radio and newspaper versions of the same news story?

Nursery children at Netley School, London, making their own "television" images.
Photo: Anne Hawes

Media texts can also be grouped *generically* (eg, soap operas, ghost stories). This makes a difference to how we read, interpret and make predictions about them. Misunderstandings, and even dislike, of media texts can often be attributed to a lack of generic understanding. Increasing the diversity of the texts that children encounter and encouraging cross-generic comparisons helps them to organise the knowledge they already have, to deal with new material more confidently and to broaden the possibilities for their own productions. A five-year-old was unable to follow the programme *Dungeons and Dragons* as it did not conform to his expectations of a drama serial. When he learned that the programme was designed as a children's quiz show he could make better sense of it.

A nine year old was able to refer to *The Goonies* as "a children's *Raiders of the Lost Ark.*"

A ten year old was puzzled by the idea of "the Force" in *Star Wars*. "What if you think of it as magic?" he was asked. "I see: then Obi wan Kenobi would be a sort of wizard" he replied, and went on to speculate fruitfully on how a science fiction film could be interpreted in fairy-tale terms.

We propose that three broad categories are useful to develop children's understanding of the media.

-    The first category is the different **media** themselves: cinema, television, etc.

-    The second category is the major **media forms:** news, fiction, documentary, light entertainment, etc. These relate particularly to producers' intentions, but also affect our expectations and understanding.

-    The third category is **genre:** westerns, romance, etc. This relates particularly to the way audiences experience and enjoy a text.

All these categories combine in any one text: *Superted* is a television programme, fiction and a superhero adventure. But any one example makes us think of other categories we might also want to use. *Superted* is a **series** (ie a succession of "one-off" episodes, as opposed to *East Enders*, which is a **serial**). It is also animated, a children's programme and it is really a parody of a superhero adventure. These categories also make a difference to the audience's understanding and pleasure, and have characteristics that link *Superted* with other series, children's programmes, animated films and parodies. Another grouping still might be by theme, eg, rescuing people.

Of course, not all texts fit easily into categories. When a film is shown on television, is it a film, or television? When we hire it on video, is it different again? How do you categorise a film like *Who Framed Roger Rabbit* which draws upon two cinema genres? Thinking about media categories must include questioning the categories, testing their boundaries and inventing new ones. The conceptually important point here is not so much knowing what category to put a text into, as understanding that putting a text into a category can make a difference to the way you think about it.

HOW HAS IT BEEN PRODUCED?
Media Technologies

Technology questions can be considered at any age and with any kind of resources. The different technologies of pencils or coloured markers make a difference to the look of a picture, and the choice between them can be discussed with very young children. Writing out a story, or word processing it, makes a difference to the look of the text and consequently can make a difference to what people think about it. Photocopying the class newspaper would cost a lot, but would reach more people. Media education should not be limited to learning "the right way" to operate costly hardware like video cameras, but needs to span the whole range of media technologies from the primitive (clay tablets, chalk and slate), to the industrial (broadcasting, newspapers).

Thinking about technology involves more than understanding and handling equipment. It links closely to the area of media agencies through issues of economics and power: who can afford to build huge sets for drama series, or to send news teams to distant countries?

It also links closely with the area of media languages. Different technologies make a difference to the meaning of a text. Children can be asked to consider, and indeed try out, how different a football match would seem when covered by one video camera, as opposed to a five-camera set-up with a *mixing desk.*

It is easy to think of media technologies as purely concerned with information and skills. These are of course important. But it is only when they are linked to the other areas of knowledge and understanding that the possibilities of media technologies come alive for children and they can see them as the tools of language.

Nursery children listening to Bengali songs on tape at Netley School, London.
Photo: Anne Hawes

HOW DO WE KNOW WHAT IT MEANS?
Media Languages

It is often assumed that visual texts in particular do not have a language: they are just "transparent" and obvious. But in fact all media forms have developed their own conventional ways of producing meanings, and children begin to learn many of these well before they start school.

Thus, a five year old showed his awareness of *cross-cutting* between simultaneous events by saying, "They're fighting on earth at the same time as they're fighting in space" and replying to the question "how do you know?" with "they changed the picture in the middle of the fight". He had gained an understanding of the convention by which cutting from one action scene to another in a drama and then back again, means "this is going on at the same time". As he got older, he would learn that this convention doesn't apply in all media or in all media forms. Cross-cutting between scenes can mean something very different in television news or arts documentary. A novel signals simultaneous events with words or phrases like "Meanwhile ..." or "While all this was going on ...".

Convention is a broad term meaning any agreed, established way in which elements of a media text can be made to refer to, symbolise or summarise particular meanings or sets of ideas. A close-up for dramatic emphasis in comics, or film and television drama, is a convention; so is the use of italics for emphasis in print. Wind, birdsong, church bells or creaking hinges are sound effects with conventional uses in radio.

When sets of conventions become fixed in a highly predictable pattern of usage - as for instance in television news bulletins or children's comics - we can call this a *code*. We *read* them effortlessly, but, just as in reading written or printed texts, our understanding depends heavily on knowledge that we bring to the text - from our own lives and from other texts. When a text works in unpredictable ways or breaks with convention, we still bring knowledge to bear on it and *make* sense of it.

It can be unproductive to make too literal a comparison between spoken and written language, and the "languages" of different media. But to think of each medium as having to some extent its own language, its own way of saying things, that we have learned, and could indeed use ourselves, is an important and perhaps central principle of media education. As we said in relation to media agencies, everything in a media text is put there on purpose and contributes to the meaning of the text, just as words do not get on to a page by accident.

Just as, in reading, we do not simply read words one by one, but constantly predict to ourselves how the rest of the sentence, the paragraph, the chapter and the whole book will turn out, so we do not read media texts image by image or sound by sound, but fit them into our constantly evolving expectations about the sort of text it is. Studying media languages includes studying the structure of media texts. Why does this shot follow that one? Will this character turn out to be a goodie or a baddie? Will there be a sad ending? Why is there a funny item at at the end of the News? Why is sport on the back pages? Why did they show the characters leaving and arriving, but not the journey in between? Why did they show that part in the flashback and not in the order in which it actually happened? Discussing how media texts are structured (whether the narrative structure of a story, the order of items on the News, or the layout of a newspaper or advertisement page) helps children to think about their own productions and other people's in a systematic way.

Most adults are so used to long-established media conventions such as close-ups, or cutting to and fro between characters in a dialogue scene, that it can be hard to think of them as elements of a language, but clearly they are learned.

"The Bash Street Kids" in the *Beano*, D.C. Thomson & Co. Ltd

In the comic strip image, the little lines behind the characters are put there to suggest speed of movement. This is so obvious that it can be hard to explain, but very young children may well ask what the lines are meant to be. Older children accept this convention as "natural".

Individual children vary a great deal in the age at which they learn to understand and utilise these conventions. Like other skills, the ability to **read** the media is probably a combination of the child's general intelligence, experience of the media, and developmental maturity. Although it is difficult to pinpoint an exact age when children become "media literate", studies suggest that most children are able to understand media conventions by the time they are eight or so, without any formal teaching. We still do not know whether children would acquire greater knowledge and understanding of media conventions at an earlier age if they received media education from the start of schooling. More research is needed on this.

Nor do we know whether children's learning of written language would be enhanced if they were encouraged to develop their understanding of media languages. (See Implications for Research, p.92).

Children's understanding of media languages can certainly be consolidated and extended systematically, through practical work in particular. Children can be encouraged to experiment with different ways of expressing their ideas, and to make decisions about which they think are most effective for their own purposes. This might entail, for example, using cardboard viewing frames or masks to decide the best way to frame an image; sequencing a set of pictures to make a story; moving a microphone to different positions in order to achieve a sense of "distance" in a sound recording; connecting a video camera to a monitor in order to try out and discuss a camera movement from one performer to another. But such work should also be supported whenever possible by studying and discussing media texts: other people's as well as the children's own. Occasionally, intensive group analysis of a limited media text such as a photograph or a title sequence is appropriate. But teachers should also work towards being able informally to note and discuss aspects of media language in the course of everyday classroom exchanges: "That's another close-up, isn't it?" "How is this picture different from that one?" "What if we listen to this bit without watching the pictures - what is the soundtrack telling us?" This kind of "media language awareness" can be encouraged from the earliest years. Teachers should recognise and exploit children's eagerness to talk about the media and be ready, when appropriate, to encourage them to reflect upon *how* they have made sense of a particular text. This is far more than "exposing the tricks" or "peeping behind the scenes" of media production. It means building up children's familiarity and confidence with media languages, so that they can both criticise them constructively and use them creatively.

WHO RECEIVES IT, AND WHAT SENSE DO THEY MAKE OF IT?
Media Audiences

The first media *audience* that a child is aware of is him or herself. Media education needs to start by enabling and encouraging children to talk about their own experience of and responses to media; Why do I like cartoons? Why do I find the news boring? Why aren't I allowed to watch *The A Team* when everyone else is?

Children develop gradually the sense of audiences other than themselves and their immediate group. They learn to imagine different audiences who might understand a text differently, and to think about how they might produce texts for audiences not known to them personally. Media education can contribute to these processes. Even a small group discussing a media text can come up with a range of interpretations: thinking about these and about why they are different is more productive than seeking a consensus or singling out a "right answer". Age, gender, class and race, as well as personal history, can all affect interpretations. Making a text for an actual and specific audience, such as younger children, can give children additional motivation and intensify the decision-making process, as the National Writing Project has shown.

Thus children can develop a sense of how texts may be made with the aim of appealing to different types of audience. In considering "types of audience", concepts of stereotyping can be introduced by investigating what media producers think is suitable for:

- women
- children
- men

- poorer people
- richer people
- black/white people
  and so on.

Children can also be encouraged to consider such questions as television *scheduling* and how media consumption relates to other areas of life eg.

- Why are women's programmes shown in the afternoon?
- Why are children's programmes shown between 4 and 5.30 pm?
  Do *you* find this convenient?
- Who might be watching TV very late at night/early in the morning?   etc.

Investigating audience entails thinking about how audiences are reached. How do you get people to take notice of what you are saying? What sort of techniques might you use, and what sort of techniques do media producers use, to attract and keep attention? (eg, big headlines, attractive photos, music on soundtracks, etc.)

This again leads to economic and technological questions: how do you get into print, or on television? How do audiences get to know about a new book or film? Publicity and marketing can be explored here; not only from the media producers' point of view, but also from the audience's. How do audiences make choices about their media consumption? Investigating that question, through such devices as reading and/or viewing diaries or a class survey, can introduce children to the problems and pitfalls of audience research. What do terms like "watching", "reading", "viewing" or "listening" actually mean? Who makes the decisions at home about what tapes to hire or which programmes to view? Which page do you turn to first in a newspaper? In which room(s) is there a television set? Children can be encouraged to think of themselves as not necessarily, or always, an undifferentiated part of a mass audience, and to recognise their own powers as active, critical consumers.

It is a difficult but exciting concept to grasp, that the effects of a text may be different from the producers' intentions. It may be resisted, subverted or misunderstood; individuals may differ in their responses. Through exploring and sharing their own responses to their own texts, children can develop a sense that results are never entirely predictable and are often very hard to identify or describe. In particular, they should be examining and challenging the popular notion of simple cause-and-effect results (eg "Television makes people passive/violent/well-informed, etc.").

In common with other areas of the humanities, children can seek to describe their personal responses to media texts and to understand those of others; including aesthetic judgements, emotional responses, and the train of ideas that a media text may inspire.

Children at Kettlebridge Nursery First School, Sheffield, watching a video of their choice. Photo: Sue Van Noort

HOW DOES IT PRESENT ITS SUBJECT TO US?
Media Representations

Representation can be a difficult and contentious area to teach, or even to discuss. In our view this often happens because it is conceptualised too narrowly. The exploration of how texts present their subject matter, how they relate to the real world, get reduced to questions about truth, bias, racism or sexism. These are important questions. But they are hard to answer and can easily be counter-productive when they are not considered in the broader context of representation. This in turn needs to be related to the other five areas of knowledge and understanding.

Representation is concerned with a three-way relationship:

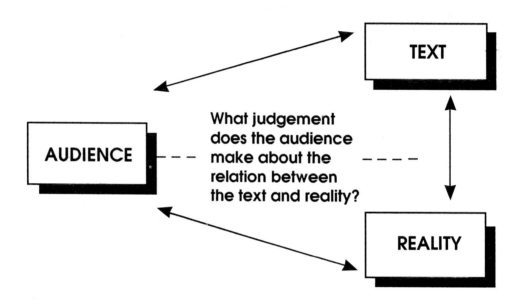

The audience's judgement will depend on their experience of, and views about, the "reality" (people, events, places, ideas, etc) that is represented in the text. It will also depend on the way they perceive the text (and perhaps who made it, how they get to see/hear/read it, its production values - indeed the whole range of questions we have discussed so far).

This may seem conceptually very abstract, but most commonplace observations about media texts are concerned with just this relationship, for example:

> I look terrible in that photograph!
> The toys look different in the advert.
> It was just like real life.
> I know it was a daft story but you could really understand how she felt.
> It just looks like they're posing.

As children get older, they can understand and investigate more of the complex questions that this three-way relationship raises, eg, what is "reality" anyway? But this is not to say that very young children cannot get a purchase on this area. In fact it can be argued that thinking about just how "real" a text is may be a major preoccupation for children.

In making judgements about representations, we all, including children, have an implicit standard about the nature of reality in our minds, based on our own knowledge and experience (or lack of it). Media representations will be measured (usually unconsciously) against this standard and found either convincing, or wanting. Media education about representation will thus inevitably give rise to considering how valid our own subjective standards of reality are, and whether our way of seeing the world is more, or less, consonant with reality than the media's.

Sometimes the media may be "right" (closer to the truth) and we may be "wrong" (further away from it). Media can be used to try to extend viewers' own limited perceptions of reality, for instance the use of counter-stereotyping about male and female roles in children's programmes such as *Rainbow*. Colin in *EastEnders* is an example of how a media representation of a homosexual is arguably more consonant with the reality of homosexual experience, than many viewers' perceptions of homosexuals, even though he is "only" a fictional character and the viewers are "real".

> *Batman is running, he makes me laugh. He eats magic things that help him to fly. He is only pretend on T.V., but he is a real person (not a cartoon). He doesn't kill people. Oliver 5yrs.*

As soon as children start to talk about the media they show an interest in the relation between text and reality. Reality is not only about perceiving events in the real world. It is also about the emotional reality of imagined events: what would be likely to happen and how we would feel about it, if these imagined events took place. The death of a character in a story may be "only pretend", but it can still make us cry. The Gremlins are only puppets, but they are still frightening. Film of an accident in the News is real, and is consequently frightening in a different way. Talking about the different levels of realism in different texts - or even within the same text - forms a good foundation for later exploring the more difficult questions of representation and stereotyping. Thinking about who represents whom, and in whose interests, and who benefits, and who doesn't get represented, brings in all the other areas of knowledge that we have been describing. It is not enough to identify sexist or racist images and condemn them. Children also need to learn how to account for such images to relate them to their contexts, how to challenge them and, where appropriate, how to replace them.

Older children can also begin to investigate questions of what, if anything, would never be represented in any medium. Issues such as censorship, taste, and propaganda would all arise here. So would questions about press freedom, investigative journalism, and the public's "right to know".

Summary of the Areas of Knowledge and Understanding in Media Education

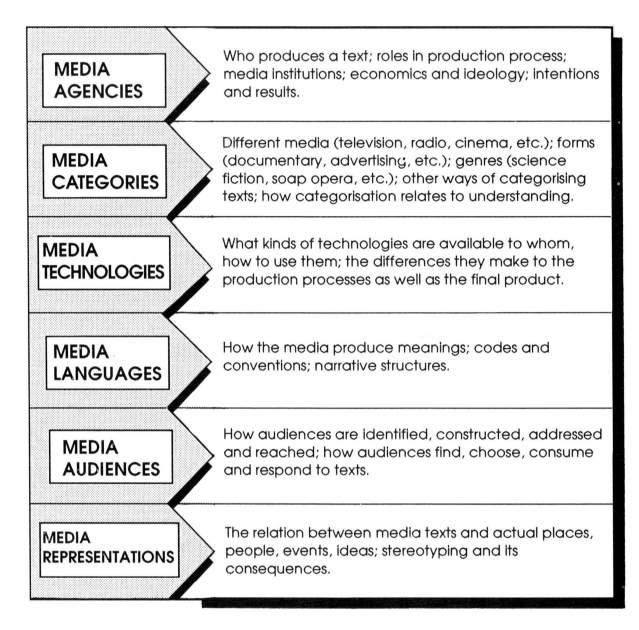

MEDIA AGENCIES	Who produces a text; roles in production process; media institutions; economics and ideology; intentions and results.
MEDIA CATEGORIES	Different media (television, radio, cinema, etc.); forms (documentary, advertising, etc.); genres (science fiction, soap opera, etc.); other ways of categorising texts; how categorisation relates to understanding.
MEDIA TECHNOLOGIES	What kinds of technologies are available to whom, how to use them; the differences they make to the production processes as well as the final product.
MEDIA LANGUAGES	How the media produce meanings; codes and conventions; narrative structures.
MEDIA AUDIENCES	How audiences are identified, constructed, addressed and reached; how audiences find, choose, consume and respond to texts.
MEDIA REPRESENTATIONS	The relation between media texts and actual places, people, events, ideas; stereotyping and its consequences.

These areas of knowledge and understanding cannot be separated from one another and must be taught about in terms of how they relate to each other. Thus they cannot form the basis for the stages of a scheme of work, though they may help to prioritise different emphases at different times. Other accounts of media education may use different terms to describe the areas of knowledge and understanding or may group them differently; there is however a broad consensus about the areas that media education should cover. Much work remains to be done in refining and clarifying these areas. This is best done through the sharing and discussion of classroom practice.

5 PROPOSED ATTAINMENT TARGETS FOR MEDIA EDUCATION

Proposed attainment targets in these six areas are outlined in the following pages. We do not think that there has been enough breadth of experience in primary media education for us to be able to set these out in terms of the ten levels of attainment recommended by the Task Group on Assessment and Testing. While we agree with such an approach (as opposed to age-related targets), we think it would be counter-productive to stipulate at this stage too much detail on how learning about the media ought to progress in the primary phase. Under each area of knowledge and understanding, we have therefore indicated two main levels of attainment, headed Level 3 and Level 5.

By doing this we are suggesting that, if children were to follow a programme of study in media education from the age of 5 to the age of 7, we would expect most of them to have attained much of the knowledge, understanding and skills outlined under the Level 3 heading. We have divided this outline into two columns. The left hand column reflects aspects of performance; the right hand column indicates knowledge and understanding.

Similarly, we are suggesting that if children continue to follow a programme of study in media education from 7 to 11, we would expect most of them to have attained much of the knowledge, understanding and skills outlined under the Level 5 heading. This outline is similarly divided into two columns.

It will be seen that, by comparison with the Subject Working Party reports for the National Curriculum, this is a limited sketch. We offer it as a basis for discussion and, in particular, as a basis for further work by teachers towards devising appropriate programmes of study, and refining these attainment targets.

MEDIA AGENCIES

Level 3

Performance

Know ways of finding out source(s)/authorship of text (eg credits, title pages, labelling).

Be able to offer description of basic production roles (eg writer, director, camera operator etc.).

Co-operate in a group, under adult direction, to produce a media text (eg sound tape, tape-slide, video, cartoon strip etc), re-drafting where appropriate.

Produce their own media text individually (eg photograph, poster, optical toy) and make decision about intended audience.

Make decisions about how to circulate a text to a number of people (eg noticeboard, photocopier, photograph, sound tape etc.)

Knowledge & Understanding

Know that media texts are produced by people: some by individuals, some by groups.

Know that media production may involve many different roles, working co-operatively.

Know that there are different ways in which a text can reach numbers of people

Level 5

Performance

Be able to identify and describe the main roles listed in film, TV and video credits, title pages, packaging.

Be able to offer description of less "visible" production roles eg producer, publisher.

Be able to identify major media institutions (eg BBC, ITV companies, local radio stations, national and local newspaper publishers, book publishers etc.)

Co-operate in a group without close adult supervision to produce a media text (eg sound tape, video, tape-slide), re-drafting where appropriate.

Make decisions about how to circulate a text to an audience not known to them personally (eg printing/local sale, local newspaper, radio).

Make editorial decisions (eg shortening or extending a text as necessary; including or excluding material on grounds of taste, tact, clarity etc); and be able to argue for and against such decisions.

Make predictions about the results of producing a particular text (eg profit, publicity, opinion-changing etc.)

Be able to speculate about producers' intentions.

Knowledge & Understanding

Know that many media texts are produced by media institutions, involving many stages of production and complex decision-making processes.

Begin to understand the processes by which texts reach large numbers of people (eg an understanding of what broadcasting is, without knowing technical detail).

Begin to understand the differences in cost and status between simple production (eg pen and paper, photographs), complex production (eg video, printing) and industrial production (eg broadcasting, mass publication).

Know how to address and reach media producers (eg how to write a letter to a newspaper or to the Advertising Standards Authority; how to telephone a television company).

MEDIA CATEGORIES

Level 3

Performance

Be able to differentiate in some way between different media: cinema, television, video, radio, books, newspapers.

Be able to identify media forms: news, drama, fiction, advertising, light entertainment (not necessarily using these terms).

Be able to identify some major genres, eg soap opera, superhero adventure, ghost stories.
Effect a transfer from one medium to another (eg illustrate a written story with photographs; make a sound tape of class news items).

Knowledge & Understanding

Understand that any media text can be categorised in a number of different ways (ie *Star Wars* is film, fiction, space fantasy).

Begin to understand some of the factors that govern differentiation between categories, eg cinema is different from radio because they use different technologies, and are used by audiences in different ways; News is different from drama because it is supposed to tell you what has really happened, etc.

Level 5

Performance

Be able to differentiate accurately between media.

Be able to differentiate most forms of media text, eg news, news and comment, documentary, dramatic reconstruction etc.

Be able to differentiate and discuss points of difference between genres, eg situation comedy, soap opera.

Be able to identify period differences in media texts.

Select and justify choice of medium, form and genre for their own production.

Effect a transfer from one category to another (eg re-tell a fictional story as news; make a superhero adventure as comedy).

Be able to identify and discuss some different characteristics of media, form and genre; to express and account for preferences.

Knowledge & Understanding

Begin to understand the technological and institutional differences between media (ie what is needed to make a sound tape for school assembly, as opposed to what is needed to broadcast a sports event internationally).

Understand that a text originated in one medium may reach its audience in another (eg films may be seen in a cinema, on broadcast television, or on video).

Understand that each medium has to some extent its own specificity and language (eg a film is not the same on television as it is in the cinema; a story is not the same in a book as it is in a film).

MEDIA TECHNOLOGIES

Level 3

Performance

Be able to identify simple technological differences between and within media forms (see CATEGORY), eg distinguish between cinema and television and between live action and animation.

Make decisions about the use of available media technologies eg felt tip/paint; photograph/drawing; and be able to discuss and justify choices made.

Operate basic equipment: paint brush, audio cassette player, auto-focus still camera, pinhole camera, video recorder, keyboard etc.

Use cardboard frame to plan composition of image; frame a subject as intended, using still, video or cine camera.

Be able to speculate on ways and means of achieving special effects.

Knowledge & Understanding

Understand that technological choices make a difference to the meaning of a text.

Understand principles of:

- persistence of vision (eg flick books, *zoetropes*)

- magnification and projection

- mirror reflections and printing

- positive and negative images

Understand that categories and forms also affect our expectations and understanding of a text.

Level 5

Performance

Be able to identify different characteristics of a wide range of media technologies (eg in animation: drawn, cut-out, computer, three-dimensional and painted on film).

Operate a range of media technologies: still camera, word processor, video camera, audio recorder, cine camera, microphone.

Recognise common technological effects, eg *chromakey*, echo effects.

Be able to plan, draft and prepare graphics for video or a simple page layout for a newspaper, magazine or book.

Be able to undertake simple assembly editing of sound tape, film or video; be able to log material taped or filmed, and plan final edit.

Be able to predict and describe the outcomes of technological choices (both actual and hypothetical), according to what is available, through school purchases or loan, eg using slides rather than photographs, or using two video cameras rather than one.

Knowledge & Understanding

Understand what differences technological choices make to the meaning of a text.

Have experience of using and discussing a range of media technologies (range is more important than complexity of equipment).

Be aware of the fact that technologies have changed over time, and continue to change.

MEDIA LANGUAGES

Level 3

Performance

Be able to observe, identify and discuss features of audio/visual texts, such as:

- different camera angles and distances*

- arangement of people and objects within the frame*

- different sounds and levels of amplification*

- colour, black and white, variations in colour tone, light and dark, sharp and soft focus

- different transitions from shot to shot (eg fade, dissolve, *cut, wipe*)

- camera movements (eg *pan, tilt, dolly* and *zoom*)

- variations in writing, print size and typeface*

- variations in size and quality of paper*

* Be able to deploy these purposefully in their own texts.

Recognise as conventions certain features of media forms and genres (eg who speaks direct to camera and who does not; how invisible "effects" such as speed, impact etc are shown in comic strips).

Follow and comprehend a simple narrative structure.

Be able to identify and discuss structuring features such as music, special effects, location, interior/exterior settings, actors, presenters, commentators.

Be able to distinguish between presenting (eg reading the news, announcing a programme) and acting (eg playing a role in a drama or an advertisement).

Knowledge & Understanding

Understand that all parts of a media text have meaning and were put there on purpose (ie that texts are constructed).

Begin to understand the concept of convention.

Begin to understand that objects may be used symbolically or indicatively (eg a Rolls Royce may symbolise wealth).

Level 5

Performance

Be able to identify and discuss how conventions are used in media texts (eg speech bubbles and frames in comics; headlines, photographs and captions in newspapers; zooms, cuts, wipes and dissolve in film and television).

Be able to follow and discuss editing procedures in film and television and to identify and discuss how space and time can be altered to tell a story.

Be able to plan, draft and story-board an audio-visual text.

Be able to imagine and experiment with modifying and breaking conventions.

Recognise and describe some historical changes in media conventions.

Be able to deploy purposefully most of the features listed in column 1 (according to available technology).

Be able to explain or hypothesise plausibly why particular features of a text were selected, eg music, locations, setting, actors, *voice-over,* typeface, layout, sound effects, etc.

Speculate on consequences of choosing different features.

Identify and describe symbolic use of objects.

Begin to express aesthetic judgements of media texts.

Knowledge & Understanding

Understand the concept of convention.

Understand that each media form has to some extent its own specific language, that has developed over time, and will continue to develop, and that we learn these languages.

Understand the basic principles of editing: that the meaning of a text can be altered by:

- deleting parts

- adding parts

- altering the sequence of parts.

MEDIA AUDIENCES

Level 3

Performance

Be able to express and discuss their media responses, preferences and reasons for them, eg pleasure, boredom, anger, puzzlement, fear, excitement, disapproval, identification.

Be able to suggest ways in which they could find out about media products (eg continuity announcements, trailers, advertisements, packaging, word of mouth, TV and film listings, promotional coverage).

Undertake simple surveys of media consumption amongst people they know (eg class viewing diaries) and use bar or pie charts to show results [correlate with attainment targets in science and maths].

Produce a media text for a specific audience (eg a poster for parents; a "newspaper" for the classroom wall).

Knowledge & Understanding

Understand that different people's understanding of and pleasure in a text can vary; and that this variation may relate to social group (eg age or gender).

Understand that the decision to address a particular audience will affect what goes into a text and how it is presented and circulated.

Understand that media texts are usually directed to audiences that the producers do not know personally.

Level 5

Performance

Be able to hypothesize responses in audiences they do not know personally.

Undertake surveys of media consumption and draw conclusions from the results.

Be able to compare texts directed to different audiences (eg *Newsround* and *Nine O'clock News*) and suggest reasons for differences and similarities.

Produce a text for an audience other than themselves (eg a book for younger children; a video for parents of prospective pupils).

Identify and compare different contexts for media consumption: cinema, home, street, school, etc.

Knowledge & Understanding

Know about:

- ratings and readership figures and what they signify

- censorship and debates about it.

Understand that different factors can affect audience readings: social class, economic status, educational background, race, gender and age, as well as personal experience.

Understand that different contexts for media consumption can affect the meaning of a text for audiences, eg where it's seen/heard, who with, when, etc.

Understand that media texts are often intended for specific audiences (eg as defined by market research).

MEDIA REPRESENTATIONS

Level 3

Performance

Make judgements about different levels of "reality" in media texts, discuss these with others, and explore what is meant by "real", eg *The A Team* is more real than *Bugs Bunny* because it has real people in it, but it's not as real as the News.

Recognise differences in representations of the same objects or people in different texts, eg Roland Rat and the Pied Piper show rats differently.

Make choices about how to represent themselves and other people in a media text (eg photograph), in terms of:

- size of figure in frame

- dress, background, hairstyle

- camera angle

- expression, position, etc.

Be able to analyse and comment on results in terms of:

- reaction to producers' intentions

- reaction to what subject is thought to be "really like".

Knowledge & Understanding

Understand that a media text is necessarily different from the places, people or events it represents ....

....and that this difference will vary in kind and extent according to many factors including:

- producers' intentions, eg we won't show the broken windows in our *tape-slide* because we want to give a good impression of the school.

- the medium, form and genre, eg animated cartoons can show a cat getting squashed flat and it's funny, but a live action film wouldn't show it.

- technology available, eg we can't make a clear recording of everyone who speaks in a class discussion, if we only have one fixed microphone.

- intended audience, eg they don't show frightening things on the News at six o'clock because young children might be watching.

.... and that audiences will make different judgements about texts (see AUDIENCE).

Level 5

Performance

Be able to represent objects, people or events from various points of views using a variety of media.

Be able to represent different emotional states in media texts.

Identify and discuss differences in representations of objects, people or events in different texts, and be able to account for these.

Be able to present a case against stereotypical representations when appropriate, and propose changes.

Be able to use the terms "represent" and "representation", as in "we made two tape-slides; one represented the school as very nice and the other represented it as a horrible place."

Knowledge & Understanding

Begin to understand the term "representation" as a way of describing the relationship between text and "reality".

Understand some of the reasons for audiences making different judgements about how texts relate to reality (eg white people may think it a good thing that the media show black people as good at sport; black people may be angry that their achievements in other fields are not shown.)

Begin to understand that it may be necessary to use stereotypes in media texts, eg comic strips are pleasurable partly <u>because</u> they show simple predictable characters, or a story might have a sexist character in it in order to criticise sexism.

TEACHING APPROACHES

Introduction

Much work remains to be done in devising coherent programmes of study for media education at the primary level. Very few teachers have had the opportunity to teach about the media consistently and systematically over extended periods of time. Where this has happened, it appears that the effect is beneficial across the whole curriculum, and not just in terms of the attainment targets proposed in the previous section.

It is noticeable that, where teachers have gained enough confidence with the areas of knowledge and understanding, the decision is usually made to integrate media education fully with the curriculum. This does not mean that they do not still undertake explicitly "media" topics, but that in addition, the "media" aspects of any topic will be taken up where appropriate. This may mean a range of approaches, from informally commenting on the illustrations in story books or poster, to including an investigation of the media elements of a topic. Teachers who are new to media education will probably experiment with well-defined short term projects or topics, from which they can gain an understanding of where such work might lead.

This Curriculum Statement, as we have already said, is intended to stimulate, and help to structure, the classroom work and relections upon it, that will lead to programmes of study. We therefore want to offer here a few examples of teaching approaches which illustrate the range of current primary media education practice. These are drawn from a number of sources, including the Working Papers from the National Working Party. We cannot offer a comprehensive description of every kind of practice, so the following must be regarded as a limited sample.

Batman goes somewhere, the baddies come, Batman and Robin fall down. Supergirl gives him a tablet, he is kind and goodlooking, I would love to go on an adventure with him. It's a film at breakfast time, it's happening. He gets ready whilst the man reads the news. He's not an actor.

Making a Start

For many schools, access to a range of media materials can be difficult. Copyright restrictions currently forbid showing tapes of general output television in schools; obtaining a full-length film to show in school, or taking a group to the cinema is expensive and time-consuming. Although we recommend that media education include children's involvement with all media forms, we recognise that starting with freely available material, such as photographs, and relatively accessible resources, such as still cameras, can be a good way to build both teachers' and childrens' confidence with new areas. The following examples show how three teachers set about starting work with photographs and photography.

Close Study of Images

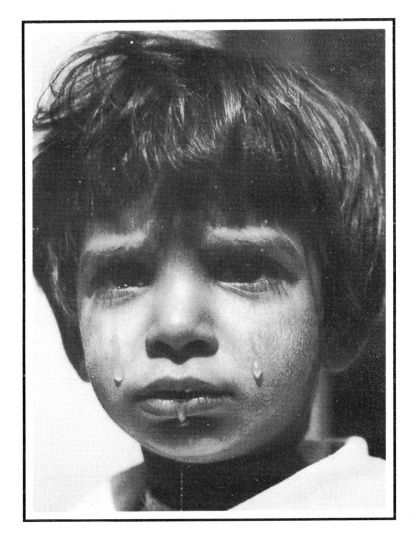

Photo: Werner Bischof
Hungary 1947

"When you've looked at the slide, I want you to note down what you remember most about the image. It might be something happening, or it may be the colour or a particular mood in the slide. Then I'll show the slide again and ask you to note down the second most memorable thing."

It's a Wednesday afternoon in the assembly hall-dining room. 36 ten and eleven year olds space out on the floor, eyes towards the empty white rectangle on the opposite wall. After the first slide we read round reporting what we now know to be the main visual clues. Most of the class have "eyes", "tears" or "crying" written down.

"Why do you think that was the most memorable thing about the first slide? Can you say more about it?"

"Well, the eyes are important, I mean they're looking straight at you."

"What are they telling you then?"

"Sadness. He looks lonely, upset, as though something awful has happened."

"Yes. Something terrible, like he could be starving or been in a disaster."

"His parents could've been killed, I think, 'cos he's coloured and he looks like the children and victims you see on the news and that."

Continuing with the exercise the children began to recognise the constant consensus of opinion about the main visual clues as significant of an underlying "image" language. My aim in introducing the slides to the whole class in this way was to encourage accurate, concentrated observation and emphasise that images can "speak", underlining the how and why of the visual clues focused upon. The children's answers mirrored the image code which society, our Western society, deals in, ie, a black child crying can be seen as an under-privileged viticim, even though, as it turns out, this picture is of a Hungarian child, a member of a children's gang. The skill of decoding images is one in which primary children are fluent given the opportunity and environment in which it can thrive.

I followed up this initial class exercise with some study of images in small mixed-ability groups. My aim each time was to enhance the children's way of looking at images by decoding the features to show how they had been constructed. The assignments involved a range of valuable language skills including describing, recording, logical reasoning and predicting, and was both written and oral. They did not all complete the same assignments, so the feedback to the rest of the class became an integral part of each exercise as the notion of "audience" was extended.

One group examined the images from local papers without the text. Their assignment was to imagine a caption for the image, then the story behind it. The images were mounted and displayed with the children mainly choosing to imitate the standard newspaper lay-out format associated with the local press. In discussion with other groups afterwards, some of the captions were challenged and had to be justified; sometimes rival stories for the same image were focuses for the best decoding of an image. On the whole this afforded a wealth of material since the photographs were rather ambiguous. The only exception was the pin-up of this year's Dairy Queen elected by Shropshire Young Farmers. Consequently the children's captions and stories were far removed from the original. For example, a group of protestors next to a barricaded footpath were not seen as "enraged residents", but as a group of neighbours about to go on an organised coach trip, a family reunited after several years apart, and some people who wanted their photograph taken as it was one of the first sunny days of the year. We talked about the reasons for such discrepancies. The children's answer was firstly that the locals were so pleased to be photographed that they had all smiled at the camera, and secondly that the photographer had not been particularly clever if he was trying to show a group of "enraged" residents.

Another group examined the images surrounding one event only, the C.N.D. rally in Hyde Park, and discussed differences in emphasis. Another compared slides of the *TV Times* and *Radio Times* covers depicting Princess Anne and Mark Phillips. A final group looked at long shots and close-ups using slides and photographs from environment study trips during the year and selected shots from the teaching pack "The Visit". I was forced to use still images at this stage for the practical reason that we have a very limited access to video or film equipment. Even had this not been the case, I would have begun in a very similar direction so that the children could decode the image without the added complexity of camera-angle changes, lighting, sound, etc.

From this small beginning the class became extremely interested in looking in greater detail at images and recording their ideas.

from "Understanding Images" by Yvonne Davies in "Beginning Media Studies in the Primary School", BFI Advisory Document, 1983.

Batman helped my dog from drowning. He did something magical. He went underwater and flew back up and gave him back to me. He is real on the tele. He is only on the tele. He lives inside.
Rachelle   3 yrs.

Taking Portrait Photographs

I teach a class of 22 children aged 5-7 years in an inner city Sheffield school. Only four children in this class speak English as a first language; languages spoken in the homes of the other children include Punjabi, Pushto, Urdu, Bengali, (Sylheti dialect), Arabic and Irish travellers' dialect.

Most of the children are beginning to read, and like many first schools we had alphabet wall friezes in their classrooms as teaching aids to phonic work. I found commercially produced alphabet friezes inappropriate to the needs of this class. The illustrations for specific sounds were often to objects unknown to the children, confusing rather than clarifying the issue. For example, K for Kangaroo, I for Igloo. We decided to make our own alphabet frieze, the children taking photos of each other, K for Kirin, I for Irfan.

I had another motive for suggesting that the children photograph each other. This term (Spring 86) a school photographer took portrait type photographs of the children, both children and parents were delighted with the photographs, but devastated at the price charged for them - few parents in this school have employment, few could afford to buy them. I intended, if the photos taken for the wall frieze turned out well, to sell copies to parents at 10p over cost price.

This would:

a   provide cheap photos of their children to disappointed parents who had been unable to afford the professional photographers' school portraits.

b   help to finance, through a very modest profit, the purchase of more camera film for this class to use.

c   interest the parents in the work this class have been doing this term with cameras, enticing them into the class to see the wall frieze, in effect an exhibition of the children's work, photos of the children, by the children.

d   to introduce to the children the idea of professional photography, of making a living through taking successful photographs that people would want to buy, initially through the concept of the school photographer, and through a discussion of why school photos were so expensive when our own school photos were not.

We used an Olympus Trip and colour film. The children planned and took all the photographs themselves from A for Andrew to Z for Zanik. We could not find anybody in the school whose name began with X. This was our only problem.

The children worked in pairs, photographer and subject. They negotiated the choice of background (the house corner, a wall display, the book corner, etc) and whether the subject should be photographed full-face, profile, head and shoulders or whole body. This involved a lot of skills, confidence with the camera, planning, decision-making and lots of language work. All the photographs were taken indoors using a flash, all the photos have proved successful enough to use for the purpose for which they children intended them - our own alphabet wall frieze, but also an exhibition of children's work, using a camera in the first school.

The predominance of non-English speaking children in the class inflected my work towards visual production. Using the photographs as an alphabet frieze linked the work to phonics. They also aided social integration, by helping children to remember each other's names. The activity strengthened links with parents.

I invited the children to identify photographs that "didn't work" and to discuss why. The packaging of the professional product had impressed the children and added to their disappointment at being unable to afford them. But when the children took these photographs by themselves, in pairs, there was a noticeable difference between the kind of poses used, and the conventional/tense poses adopted for the "school photo".

from "Photography" by Sue Van Noort, in "Working Papers One", BFI Education 1986.

More Portrait Photographs

Taking a mixed group of 3rd and 4th year juniors, we started to explore using photography as a communication tool. Most of the class knew me well already and had at least used cameras on school journeys a couple of times with me, and some had their own. They took to the idea of developing a photography topic that term and I started by asking them to compose a photo. I was going to take a photograph of each of them using black and white film (economy and choice on my part). I wanted them to decide where in school they wanted the photo taken, to say if they wanted head and shoulders, profile, whole body, to be holding anything, etc. I was interested in the image they had of themselves, what kind of image they thought their photo would project and what they thought when they saw the result. Indeed many were quite surprised at what they looked like. Nearly all were pleased for some reason or other. Some looked quite mature and were pleased about that; some actually tried to create that image. Two did, and one girl who in class and personality was generally immature, was amazed and didn't recognise herself in the photo. The day the photo was taken was a rare occasion when she had her hair tied in a pony-tail and she had chosen to pretend to be talking on a phone we had in class. She actually said, "Cor, is that me? I look like a secretary." She was delighted with the image. Already the group was gaining knowledge that images could be manipulated. They wrote short but informative accounts about why they had chosen to have their photos taken that way, and what they thought of the result. The giving of an "opinion" and being "critical" came automatically because of the questions asked. The words "opinion" and "result" counted so much. That their opinion counted and the importance of seeing a result of an idea/thought mattered and affected the way they reacted and wrote. At the same time I took a class photo and wrote a piece about the photo for the children to read. I wanted to gain more knowledge of the childrens' frustration about writing, so I did it with them, suffering under the same conditions and pressure. It was hard! I completed it after much scratching out at the draft stage and three attempts at copying out with my pen. I found it hard to communicate my thoughts on paper.

The children made books to keep their photos and writing in and looked forward to the second activity which involved them taking photographs themselves. By now with all this interest in photography, I was a proud owner of an SLR camera which I used to take the photos of them and often had in class for them to hold and practice focusing with. We had started together quite a collection of old cameras that children and friends donated, so the children really did get quite used to "framing" a photo. We also started to draw them, label the parts and build up an extensive vocabulary of words and read up more about how a photograph is produced. (A few had the opportunity to develop and print through school journey work.)

So on they went to take photos themselves, using Instamatics and colour film (their choice) of things they chose. Most chose to take photos of groups of friends, other plants and animals in the classroom. The organising of their friends and objects for the photos amused them and me greatly and provoked a lot of discussion and collaboration. They knew what they wanted and did actually co-operate quite well with one another. Again when it came to writing they were asked - why did you choose to take the photo like this and are they satisfied with the result. How could you improve it?

from "Learning Photography" by Sheila McGlade in "Beginning Media Studies in the Primary School", BFI Education 1983.

Through more extended work with a number of teachers, a London advisory teacher was able to draw up a broader cross-curricular plan for photographic work which other teachers could follow.

Developing Photography

The camera is being used more and more as a means of recording events in the school calendar - outings, school journeys, fetes and other special occasions. But what do these photographs say about the school? Are they a realistic representation of the fete? Do they show how hard everyone in the school worked to produce the play, or just the people on stage? What does it show about our values if we only have pictures of winners on sports day?

Children are confronted with still images every day, from family or school snapshots to pictures in information books and print advertisements. We need to guide children towards an understanding of the power of the photographer has in relation to what is deliberately put into or left out of a picture, the angle from which it is taken and the distance it is taken from. The influence of the photographer does not stop here. When the photographs have been developed a choice can be made from a selection, or a picture cropped to reflect something in a particular way. By taking on the role of the photographer and by working with all kinds of images throughout their school lives, children will begin to appreciate and understand these issues.

Talking about Images
Ask children to bring two images from home (photographs, magazine pictures, newspaper clippings), one of something they really like, the other something they don't like.

Have a selection of school snapshots, magazine and newspapers available in the classroom for those children who may have difficulty in bringing something from home. Encourage the children to share their feelings about the images with a group of friends. Prompt them by asking where they think they were taken. When was it? What do they like/dislike about it? What does it make them think about?

This should begin to make them aware that they have different preferences and opinions. You may need to intervene and support them with this discussion.

Thinking Photographers
Before even picking up a camera it is important for children to carry out a variety of activities which encourage them to look carefully at what they see within a frame. Take an A4 sheet of thin cardboard and cut out a regular shape from the middle - circle, square, rectangle or triangle - to give the impression of looking through a camera viewfinder.

Let the children have fun experimenting with irregular shapes as well.

Make this an art activity by asking the children to look at every detail of an image through these clear frames and then represent it as clearly as possible on a piece of paper. The variety of choice highlights how we can construct an image in a particular way by including or excluding certain things in the frame.

First Photographs

Children need to understand certain basic technical aspects of photography:

- Remember that the camera is a delicate piece of equipment

- Always stand still when you're taking a picture

- Never point the camera into the sun.

Some of their early attempts may not look quite as they intended. Prepare them for this and use it as a learning point.

Use a class outing as a chance for the children to take a variety of photographs which remind them of the day. They should take at least three photographs each. While some are taking pictures others could use frames to plan their images.

When the photographs have been developed, talk together about what the photographs as a whole say about the outing. Ask the class to select photographs which depict the outing in a certain way - as fun, tiring, boring, interesting, and so on.

Display the images with captions. Some children may like to crop their photographs to show that they could fit in more than one section. Show them how to do this by covering parts of the image with paper. Using their own photographs in this way helps children to realise how images can be manipulated.

Take the activity further by asking the children to think about what they left out of their photos and whether or not this changes the reading of them. This is preferably carried out as an art activity. The children place the photograph of their choice anywhere on a larger piece of paper and fill in the missing surround. See if they can change the image by inventing an imaginary surround. Give the class the chance to share their ideas and talk together about the images they have created.

Juniors taking photographs of each other at Stottesdon School, Shropshire. Photo: Mike Hamon

Photowalk

As the children develop more confidence in their photographic ability they should be able to think about and take photographs which show an event, a person or an environment from a particular point of view.

Working in groups the children take six or eight photographs of a walk to a particular place - the library, the swimming baths, etc.

Each group takes photographs of the same walk, but from different perspectives. These perspectives - neglected, industrial, residential, busy, etc - can be selected during class disussion.

Make sure every group has a large map of the route. The children should walk the route at least once to choose their particular images and then go out on a separate occasion to take their photographs. Mount the photographs on the maps and display them clearly in the classroom. It is a good idea for groups of older or more able children to work on a short talk about the perspective portrayed through their work.

By Fiona Collins and Sandra Newnham in "Media Education Topic Pack", Junior Education, vol 33 no 11, November 1987)

All of the preceding work, although limited to one medium (photography), develops and integrates the areas of knowledge and understanding. The children are investigating who takes photographs and why, what different categories of photograph they can devise and use, how photographs are made, how they make sense of them, what they think of them, where they see them, how they present their subject matter and how this can be inflected through framing, cropping and captioning as well as through what is chosen as the subject in the first place. This kind of work can be extended to other media, as is shown by the following examples, relating to television.

Categorisation through Talk

The following extract is taken from a transcript of a discussion I had with a reception class in an infant school in Newport, a small market town in Shropshire. The class was one of the first classes in the school containing some children of five who had been there for a term or more and others of 4+ who had attended for only a few weeks. The class teacher had attended the half day "Language and the Media" course at the local teachers' centre and I, as advisory teacher, had visited the school once before. On this occasion I had been asked to go in and talk with the children about television in connection with a general investigation of what children watch, which the in-service course was engaged in. The children barely knew me, nor did I know anything about their backgrounds or abilities. I was able to take them to a separate room as a group of eight or so at a time and I used a cassette recorder with a built-in mike. They did not seem at all inhibited at having their talk taped. The children's motivation was generally very high, probably because they were being taken out from their classroom to do something different with a visitor! Only one child in the class was temporarily without a television. Over half had more than one television and about half had VCRs.

I gave myself a specific brief, namely to find out if these children could distinguish one sort of television programme from another. Could they categorise programmes by genre? What knowledge did they have about different genres? If they could make a distinction, what kinds of language were they using to make it? Could they name the differences?

YD: Who thinks it's the same as watching *Blue Peter?* When you see a cartoon ... and when you see *Blue Peter*, is it the same? That's a hard question isn't it?

Child: It isn't the same because *Blue Peter* is a film

YD: Is it? (interested)

Child: It's a programme

YD: Someone thinks it's a film, someone thinks it's a programme, but what about Bugs Bunny, then - someone said, "Oh, it's a cartoon". What's the difference?

Child: It's s'posed to be a cartoon, 'cept it (he) has to dig holes and find carrots at the farm or he can't get * animals

Child: or, um, a man tries to come out and tries to kill him, Bugs Bunny, but, um, Bugs Bunny, he's faster than him.

In my first question I repeat a previous question to clarify their response as there were some children saying "different" and some saying "yes, yes" meaning "yes, *Blue Peter* is the same as a cartoon". In retrospect, I think I was asking an even more difficult question that I indicated at the time. Concepts of similarity and difference are high on the agenda of the primary curriculum anyway. It is therefore interesting and surprising that one child in the group is able to say almost straightaway, "It isn't the same because *Blue Peter* is a film". This seems to clarify the type of response I hoped my question would elicit. After all, we all know that Bugs Bunny is not *Blue Peter* so what is this teacher asking us for? That line of response was jettisoned by this child's statement and my "Is it?" reinforces that "programme type" is the line of inquiry that I want to pursue. The second child then immediately says "It's a programme" and the intonation of this sentence coupled with my recall of the discussion leads me to conclude that the child was providing an alternative rather than an addition, ie, *Blue Peter* is a programme rather than a film, not *Blue Peter* is a programme as well as a film. During the whole discussion these children used the term "programme" a great deal to provide a category for certain types of television. My first interpretation of this was that "programme" was a genre category for them. Now I am not so sure. They may well have understood that cartoons are programmes, *Blue Peter* was a programme, etc as opposed to a trailer, advertisement, or newsflash. There was an assumption from the beginning, because I was asking them to tell me about their favourite TV *programmes*, that not only certain sorts of television were already excluded, but maybe I hadn't even acknowledged that they existed! "Programme" is obviously a term used on television to present itself to its audience so it is no surprise that this is the one most easily used by the children. We often say, "Did you watch that programme about ...?" We do not often say, "Did you watch that Bugs Bunny programme?" meaning "cartoon". Another observation concerns the terms "film". Interesting to note that this distinction is made between a cartoon and *Blue Peter,* when it is actually the magazine programme which employs film only now and them. Yet we know that there is a common usage which makes this distinction.

Child 1:   Is *Labyrinth* a cartoon then?

Child 2:   No, it's a film.

At the end of the extract, the last two child utterances are anecdotal. At first I thought the two stories were simply the way children often tell you what they know or are interested in regardless of what I had asked. On examining the transcript more carefully, I now think that my question, "What is the difference?" which I had taken to mean, "What's the difference between a Bugs Bunny cartoon and *Blue Peter?*" was interpreted by the first child responding as "What's the difference between Bugs Bunny and a cartoon?" Hence the unexpected answer: "It's s'posed to be a cartoon, 'cept it is er ... and he has to dig holes and find carrots at the farm, or he can't get * animals".

This child tries to help me out by repeating slowly and thoughtfully that you could make a distinction between a cartoon and Bugs Bunny because a "cartoon" could possibly mean something else which does not involve a narrative structure like other cartoons. This child's particular cartoon favourites were *Thundercats, He-Man* and the *Get-Along-Gang.* Now the narrative structure of Bugs Bunny is very different from these. It is as the child says based around a general theme of haviong to dig holes, find carrots, get away from animals and this theme is played around with in short sequential bursts. *He-Man,* on the other hand, tells one story at greater length, involves many more characters and moves like a traditional narrative from a situation of harmony through a period of disruption to resolution.

From the children's discussion I think they knew and sensed the difference. The second child's response: "or, um, a man tries to come out and tries to kill him, Bugs Bunny, but, um, Bugs Bunny, he's faster than him". This backs up the first utterance by providing another example of the sort of narrative pattern found in a Bugs Bunny cartoon.

from "Talking about Different Kinds of Televison" by Yvonne Davies, in "Working Papers Four", BFI Education 1988.

Victoria and Paul, aged 6, cutting out pictures from newspapers to sort into categories. Copplestone School, Devon. Photo: Sandra Sutton

Analysing an Advertisement

At the beginning of the Spring term 1987 using a whole-school project - Communication - as a springboard, I asked my class to write about their favourite advertisment on television and to make a comic strip of the important shots. The Cherry Coke advertisement appeared to be popular with the girls. One girl wrote:

> "My favourite ad is Coke, where a girl comes and sings "I am the future of the world, I am the hope of the nation, I am tomorrow's people, I am the new inspiration". Then more and more children come and sing "We've got a song to sing to you, tomorrow, tomorrow, etc." Why I like this song is because the girl didn't have an out of tune voice. The song is not going lower and lower ... the kind of feeling they got inside without laughing and spoiling it and being embarrassed." (Sehriban)

It appeared that it was the confidence of the girls in the advertisement and the way that the girls identified age-wise that attracted them to it. Later it proved to be less popular, once the song was understood and the implications explored they were less sure that the meaning behind it really said what it should - "All that about a bottle of Coke!"

One main element that became apparent was the children's ability to take on board and to be able to sing the jingles of the advertisments without understanding or engaging in the underlying meanings and effects.

This ability to sing the lyrics to a television advertisment without understanding the values and ideas implied became more apparent when as a class we watched the Coke advertisement current in January this year. I played the video of the advertisement three times without any comment. The class thought it fascinating to watch an advertisement three times without stopping and asked me to play it time and again. They sang along with the song and asked me to stop the video at various points, when they were not sure of the meaning of the shot. We often disagreed as to the meaning. We began to realise that there were at least twenty different little scenes, which did not seem to be connected in any way. One child said that the song matched the shots, so back in the classroom we began to break down the song and match the lyrics with the shots. Each child was asked to choose a favourite shot to draw. The organisation of this proved to be difficult, as some shots were more popular than others. Eventually a list of all the different shots was put up and children put their names by whatever they wanted to draw, or failing that, their second choice. Each shot was drawn on the same size paper, so that we could connect each one for the complete narrative sequence. Whilst drawing the shot the child became aware of what filled the frame and recalled the ideas of a close-up, mid shot and long shot, from storyboards of fairy tale slide/tapes, and discussion.

Throughout the work in progress we had discussions about style, music, length, speed, clothes, gestures, expression, ideas, message, camera angles and framing. We also touched on audience in respect of the age group that this advertisement was aimed at. The time the advertisement was shown and during which programmes were also discussed. A group of girls from Bangladesh wondered why no Muslim people appeared in the advertisement and mentioned their disapproval of seeing women in swimming costumes and couples kissing. The children generally wondered why Coca-Cola needed to advertise, as it was popular anyway, and decided as a group that advertisements are usually enjoyable in themselves, ie, you can see different fashions and lifestyles that you can copy - but that sometimes you were not aware or really interested in what the companies were advertising, or why.

from "The Coke Ad. Top Juniors" by Yvonne Madley in "Working Papers Three", BFI Education 1987

A form such as advertising, which cuts across all the media, is often employed as the basis for a major class or school topic. Other examples might be news, or game shows. The following account of an extended project with top juniors shows how wide-ranging such an undertaking can be.

Extended Work on Advertising

In today's society we, children and adults alike, are surrounded and affected by the media, TV, advertising, comics, etc. As teachers we are constantly confronted by children's involvement in the media, their conversation with each other on last night's TV programmes, dramatic plays influenced by concept toys and stories created around TV characters. What other media industries are they involved in? What is their understanding of these? These questions and many more started the initial thinking around a project on advertising. The project was then carried out with a class of nine and ten year olds at Christchurch School, London, during part of the Spring Term of 1987.

The project was conceptually based and aimed to give the children an understanding of audience, construction and (to a lesser degree) representation. It was divided into two with the conceptual thinking centred in the first half and then a simulation of an advertising campaign in the second, in which the children could put into practice some of the ideas they had grasped previously. In splitting the project it was hoped the children would develop a framework to understand the industry as well as being able to stand back and question it.

In working on a media education project in this way a variety of skills were identified as being important:

-	discussion skills	-	group work skills
-	listening skills	-	critical awareness
-	problem solving	-	presentation/role play
-	questioning/challenging	-	working to a brief
-	independence	-	design

As the project progressed it was obvious that children developed these skills through the various activities and the simulation at the end.

Other curriculum areas played an integral part such as language throughout, written and oral, social studies and maths with regards to the research and surveys carried out and music in the children's advertisements.

The project actually started by allowing us and the children to look at their knowledge, understanding and involvement in this particular media industry.

Mark, aged 10,
Christchurch
School, London

My favourite advertisment

My favourite advertisment is Anchor butter. I like it because it start's off with people spreading anchor butter on some toast then a cow pokes his head out of a bush and start's singing. The camera show's you three cow's but there all the same. I think it a camera trick.

I like the advertisment because It's funny I do not like the product. There is nothing I do not like about the advertisment.

mark

What Do the Children Know and Like About Advertising?

In investigating the children's knowledge of advertising we wanted to find out if they knew the difference between a print advertisement and a photograph illustrating an article in a magazine. This investigation was carried out through a discussion in which the class were shown a variety of images. One such image was a Jaeger advertisement with a woman model lying down, ringed with pink and the only word, "Jaeger", was covered up. The children were asked whether this was a photo or an advertisement, ie selling something. The general feeling among the children was that it was an advert selling clothes, as the woman looked glamorous, she looked like a model, the colouring of the picture was unusual and that she was lying down. The class then went on to discuss a variety of advertisements and non-advertisements and the differences between them. Towards the end of the discussion the children were asked about other forms of advertising and where you would see them. Television commercials on ITV and Channel 4 were mentioned. One child said there were adverts on the BBC channels. Asked what these were she said for AIDS, and the class was then told these were for public information. The children defined the two by saying one was selling a product while the other was giving information.

From this varied and interesting discussion the children were asked to work in pairs and actually change a photograph into an advertisement. Some pairs found it difficult not to describe the picture in detail and needed help in writing short, sharp phrases actually selling something in their picture. They also had a few problems in writing co-operatively but those with difficulty were encouraged to write everything down about their picture and then think about the copy later. In this way the children were able to deconstruct the image for future reference. One pair worked with a picture of a classically good-looking white male which they changed into an advertisement for ugly cream -

> "This man used new ugly cream and look at the results! If you want to be as ugly
> as he is well pop down to your local chemist today - only 58p but hurry - offer
> ends soon."

A second pair worked with a picture of two men, surrounded by hounds on the Scottish Moors. Their main line at the top of their advertisement was "Have a jolly time in Scotland this winter." While underneath, the two men were saying to each other -

> "Were you the one who talked me into this?"

> "No it was the travel agent!"

In this way the children not only took on changing the pictures into advertisements, but also put a little humour into them as well.

After this initial series of activities the class went on to discuss their favourite adverts, which were mainly television ads. During the discussion various children described the ads they liked best, explaining why they liked them and what they actually were saying to them. One boy described his favourite, which was for Shape Yoghurt: in the advertisement a family were enjoying themselves on the beach through a variety of sporting activities, however all these were larger than life.

As the boy described the commercial he started to question what it was actually saying to him - did it mean if you eat this yoghurt you would be able to do extraordinary sporting acts, or would your life be like the family's? Other children joined in and they decided that the advertisement was stretching the truth in order to sell the product. A second child went onto describe her favourite advertisement, for an after-shave lotion. In this particular commercial an untidy man changes his appearance for the better after using a particular after-shave which goes on to affect the women in his office; they let down their hair as they see him. After telling the class about the advert the girl began to question aloud whether this particular brand of after-shave could actually do all of this for you, if you were a man that is.

Once the class had discussed their ads at length they were asked to write about them.

However, to give these descriptions some uniformity the class, as a whole, decided on the areas which should be covered:

> Description of the advertisement
> What is it advertising?
> Why do you like it?
> Is there anything you don't like?
> Do you like the advertisement or the product or both?

The favourite advertisements which were written about included:

> Anchor butter
> Shape Yoghurt
> Slim-a-Soup
> Insignia After-shave
> Chum Dog Food

In fact only one child wrote about a non-TV advertisement. After the children had finished writing they shared their work and discussed how some advertisements stated an opinion rather than including straightforward facts about the product. For instance one girl, when describing Chum dog food, wrote it was for dogs with energy and an interesting discussion followed on what did this actually mean - did it mean that dogs without energy or old dogs didn't actually like Chum dog food? The class went on to take a survey of their favourite TV advertisements and Anchor butter was the firm favourite. When talking about the result of the survey the children thought Anchor butter was their favourite because it was a fantasy advertisement and very funny.

In the week which followed this introductory session, the class surveyed the rest of the school to find out their favourite TV and poster advertisements and then drew graphs and pie charts to illustrate their results. They also decided to take a questionnaire home for their families to complete, and back in the classroom the results were collated, to show the findings clearly to everyone. This was a difficult task as some questions had been worded in such a way that there were two types of answer. However it was a rewarding exercise as the class were able to incorporate the results later on in their work.

Advertising All Around Us
The aim of this second section of work was to illustrate quite visibly to the class, how advertising pervades our lives by being on the clothes we wear, on cars, on taxis, on bags, etc. The class talked about logos on clothes and what these actually were, who had them on any item of clothing and what was the difference between a picture on the front of a T-shirt and a logo. They then went on to design their own logos which had to be personsal to them and associated with something they liked doing. Some children found this task difficult, as they wanted to put too much into the logo and as a result made them very complex. During all of this session the children constantly had to refer back to what the logo said about them, as well as considering other aspects such as colour, size, shape, style of writing, etc.

Middle Infants sorting out images on packaging into logos, writing, pictures. Wombridge School, Shropshire. Photo: Yvonne Davies

Following on from this activity the class visited the Kings Road to look at advertising in the environment. Each child wrote down any adverts they saw and on what they were advertised. The visit encouraged the children to be more observant of their surroundings. One girl became very excited when she noticed a shop called Logo which in fact she must have passed daily on her way to school without the name meaning anything to her. Back in the classroom the findings were collated in various sections, ie on what they had seen - taxis, buses, hoardings, carrier bags, etc, and questions were asked about the most visible form of advertising along the Kings Road.

Targetting

At this point in the project it was felt the class were more aware of the actual extent of advertising, what the advertisers were saying and what adverts were constructed in a certain way to sell a particular product. However the children also needed to think about target audiences and how these are defined by advertising agencies. Luckily an interested parent who worked for an advertising agency lent us a video cassette of a selection of TV commercials. The class discussed who these were aimed at and at what time they might appear on television. They also talked about the types of adverts which appear on ITV children's hour and why they are predominantly food and toy products. In relation to the food products the class thought they did actually encourage their parents to buy certain food items they had seen advertised on TV.

The class continued thinking about targetting by dividing a day's TV programmes into age categories: unders 5s, school children, teenagers, families and adults only, noting the times at which programmes in each category were shown.

The children understood the concept very quickly and were able to discuss fully the implication of being retired or unemployed with regards to day time adult viewing, ie old films on Channel 4. They then moved away from talking about targetting according to age to interest groups and how advertisers could place commercials around related TV programmes, ie they might advertise sports clothing in the breaks of an athletics meeting on a Sunday afternoon, for those viewers who not only watched sport, but were actively involved in sport as well.

Throughout the first half of the project we tried to help the children to question what they were confronted by on the television and in their lives daily, understanding the complexity of advertising and giving them a structure to make their own TV advert. More could have been covered within this section of the project, but time is always an important factor and in this instance there was not enough. However, in stating that fact perhaps a further project could have looked in more depth at such areas as :

- representation of various groups in society
- the truths of advertising promises
- the history of advertising
- packaging of products
- how television programmes sell products

The above would constitute yet another project and take the class into new and varied areas of investigation and understanding.

A Simulated Advertising Campaign

By now the children had developed some sense of how advertisements target particular groups in society, and how market research could be carried out to identify the preferences of consumer groups. They were also to find the questionnaire which they had designed for their parents useful in determining their approach to designing their own advertising campaign. We hoped that their involvement in this kind of activity would encourage the development of an understanding that advertisements are the results of a deliberate process of decision-making, selection and construction.

Briefing

As representatives of a client biscuit company we briefed the class as an advertising agency, telling them we had arranged a meeting with them because we had heard about the excellent advertising campaigns they had run for other companies. We asked them to run a campaign for us which would comprise product design, TV adverts, posters, carrier bags, packets, etc.

The product was to be a biscuit which should, as far as possible, be made with healthy ingredients and the advertising was asked to be as factual and honest as possible - to avoid "stretching the truth". (A worthwhile discussion of what kind of ingredients might be healthy took place at this stage.)

The "agency" was split into two groups each with a different target consumer group - one group was to target their campaign at 5-7 year olds and the other to target 8-11 year olds.

Planning the Campaign

To assist them in deciding on the nature of the product it was suggested that the children record their own first, second and third choice of variety of biscuit. The results of this "self-survey" was graphed by a pair of children and each group was able to use the information gained in their product design. Both groups opted for carob as a chocolate substitute and "natural" ingredients such as honey as a sweetener, wheat, nuts and sultanas etc. We had hoped that they would actually be able to make the biscuits, but lack of time precluded this activity. (One child made a clay model of star shaped biscuits at home - very realistic - which was used in her group's TV advertisement.)

Each group "brainstormed" a variety of possible names for the biscuits. These were reduced by democratic process to a shortlist of six in each case. These names were then "tested" through survey on two target groups within the school. This resulted in the choice of the name "Chew Chew Chocs" for the biscuit aimed at the 8-11 year old consumer group and "Star Biscuits" for the biscuits aimed at the 5-7 year old consumer group.

Having decided on the product name and the nature of the product, the children in each group designed storyboards for the TV commercials individually. Each child was given a duplicated sheet with spaces for drawing images and writing captions.

Once the storyboards were completed each child read and explained his/her storyboard for the other members of the group. Any storylines which represented the biscuit as being capable of endowing the eater with super power or extra strength were rapidly rejected by the other children as, making unrealistic claims for the biscuits. "Unhealthy" ingredients such as cream which turned up in some of the storyboards were also questioned and discarded.

Each group eventually came up with "composite" storyboards which utilised and combined the elements the group had liked in the storyboards made earlier with other ideas sparked off by the discussion. A strong sense of fair play operated throughout this activity and each member of the group was given a "fair hearing".

We suggested to the children that it would be useful to write a script and showed them an example of an advertising agency's script and storyboard with details of scenes, camera instructions and directions for the actors. At this stage the groups decided on the properties and costumes they would require and the detailed content of the advertisement. Sheets with points to consider in relation to this decision-making were given to the groups.

It was difficult to involve all members of each group fully in this decision-making stage. Some children did tend to dominate the groups at times and inevitably there were conflicts over whose ideas should be accepted. On reflection we felt that the groups were really too large (eleven in each group), and that ideally dividing the class into three to four groups would have encouraged individual participation in the work. Preparing the campaign involved the children in a wide variety of activities of which some were carried out individually and others in pairs or small groups. There was a considerable sense of urgency within the dynamics of the work because it all had to be fully completed and the TV advertisement rehearsed ready for videotaping in the studio the following Monday.

The nets for biscuit packets were designed, copied onto card, put together and painted. (This involved practical applications of geometry concepts and careful measurement. One group designed two cuboid shaped packets for their TV commercial, one larger and accurately produced to scale. The other group made a packet in the shape of a hexagonal prism). Placards with slogans relating to the product were manufactured using squares of thick card mounted on metre rulers. A song was written and rehearsed for one of the advertisements and for the other, accompanying music was composed and rehearsed using percussion instruments. Once the tasks related to the television advertisements were complete, work began on the making of paper carrier bags and posters with logos and slogans. (This aspect of the campaign was never fully completed as time ran out. The children's interest and concentration had by now become centred around making the television advertisement.)

During the week long simulation period, the groups regularly reported their progress back to us. Our involvement in helping them prepare the campaign was continuous. By the end of the week everything was ready (just!) and each advertisement was rehearsed (with props, costumes, music, etc.)

Videotaping

In the week prior to the simulation the class had been to the television studio at the Institute of Education, London University for a session which comprised an introduction to camera techniques and the vision-making and sound equipment. This two hour session was essentially a "hands-on" experience and culminated in the production of a short video in which a child demonstrated how to make a cup of tea while other children operated the camera, etc. This gave the children an opportunity to experiment with the effects of panning, framing and zooming and to develop some understanding of what the technology could and could not do. This experience informed the children's approach to planning their advertisements. The two advertisements were videotaped during a whole day's session.

During the preparatory activities the week before, a certain rivalry had developed between the two groups, a rivalry which we were naturally keen to discourage. However, the studio work brought the two groups together. While one group performed their advertisement, the members of the other group provided the technical crew to operate the equipment with the guidance of a "director" from the performing group and the Institute's Studio technician. Each advertisement was rehearsed then videotaped within the context of intense concentration and co-operation. Towards the end of the day however, it was noticeable that the children were becoming very tired and we felt that if we were to repeat the exercise, we would split the videotaping into half-day sessions.

from "An Advertising Project" by Fiona Collins and Peter Hart, in "Working Papers Three", BFI Education 1987.

It is not necessary for a media topic to develop from such an obviously "mass media" form as advertising. The following accounts show how the concepts of narrative and storytelling can be extended from literary study into a consideration of how they work in other media languages.

Exploring Narrative

One of the many activities happening at Chesworth School, Sussex, in last term's Bookweek, was a visit from a professional storyteller, Muriel England. To extend the meaning and enjoyment of Muriel's performance I decided to draw the attention of my class of 7-8 year olds to the power and supreme amenability of story.

We sat down and thought about what stories were important and what really was a story. Were stories about truth? If so, when was a story really true? When it was written down? Or in a newspaper?

In groups of about 5-6, I asked the children to discuss these points and relate them to a series of statements taken from Making Stories (see below), thus encouraging them to take a critical standpoint in defining a story.

With their awareness and curiosity aroused I moved the children on to considering the multi-cultural aspects of this tradition. We played a few games of whispers and the children were asked to deduce why the story that had been whispered from ear to ear to ear had transformed.

1. Stories are important to people.	8. Parents should tell their children stories.
2. Stories should be shared and passed on.	9. Everyone tells stories.
3. Only a few people should be allowed to tell stories.	10. Stories are about things that didn't ever happen but they can be true.
4. Stories belong to everyone.	11. The best stories are true stories.
5. Most people can't tell stories.	12. You can't learn anything from stories.
6. Stories are a waste of time because they aren't true.	13. The author of a story is not only the person who tells it.
7. Stories aren't true but they can be real.	14. A story can only be a proper story if it's written down.

From Making Stories by Bronwyn Mellor and Mike Raleigh with Paul Ashton, ILEA English Centre, 1984

Pondering on this, I then read them 3 stories. The first was *Snow White* (an English/European story); the second was *Hansel and Gretel* (German); the third was *Sit and Lakhan* (Bengali, Indian).

When asking the class to respond to these, their immediate comments were about how similar all three tales had been. For example, all had shared ingredients: the process of being abandoned; the wicked stepmother and the weak father. I commented on how remarkable it was that three stories from different parts of the world could be so similar.

As a class I asked if they had any explanation for these similarities. After much discussion and problem-solving the children who had continued to ponder on the whispering game arrived at one sound explanation: that possibly one story had travelled with story tellers from country to country - but, as in our game, at each step things had been changed a little. There were changes like names and customs which fitted in with a particular country.

To consolidate this explanation we raided the class's fairytale books - and giving close attention to the origins of the stories, we started to read a variety and find similarities. Very gradually the children through such a familiarisation with this genre were starting to acquire some sense of the criteria of what constituted a fairy story! This was an interesting acquisition which brought them onto a second consideration: how stories change with time.

I then read the children three versions of Cinderella: the original Chinese tale from Brothers Grimm; the Roald Dahl's "poetic" rendition and thirdly Catherine Storr's version in *It Shouldn't Happen to a Frog*. Responding to these stories was initially quite difficult, but the class started by saying how much more fun the last two were, and how boring the first one was by comparison. They liked the silly parts of the latter two, but couldn't summarise why the first one was dull. To help them I asked if *when* the stories had been written might have anything to do with it. They concluded that the first one was definitely very old - written before my time at least!

Although the children were on the verge of realising that modern day stories are for modern day kids, they hadn't really grasped why the stories were modern. The reason being that Dahl's and Storr's versions break with traditional conventions and criteria.

To help the children realise this at their own level, I then borrowed (again from the ILEA publication) a story and related work which focussed upon our expectations in a fairy story. The story was called *The Practical Princess,* but before listening to it the children were asked to respond to these predictions on an individual level. Needless to say, when the story was read out to them, most of their predictions (which had followed conventional criteria) were wrong. Easily the children concluded that the tale was modern and fun, for this reason.

The final response to this week's work was asking the children to produce their own modern day fairy story. We had all arrived at the premise that "the fun starts when things go wrong" and working from that, and with the whole week's accrued experience, they set about devising some remarkably funny stories, based on original classics. I asked them to record these, but on reflection I would dispense with this as it can slow down and hamper many of the children's creativity and originality. Perhaps we could use audio cassettes next time.

Although I am pleased that the children enjoyed the week so much, my real sense of achievement came with the children's "developed" critical response to each other's stories - picking out the classic and identifying the convention(s) which had been smashed. It has also given me some interesting ideas of how to carry this work on - for example, learning to see two sides to a story, or exploring a classic story from an alternative character's angle. Both of these potential follow ups can be remarkably sophisticated, but with Bookweek's experience behind them, I think the class will find them enjoyable, challenging considerations.

by Kathy Macdonald in "Media Education in Primary Schools 2" (occasional papers for teachers of English in West Sussex, Horsham Professional Centre, Clarence Road, Horsham, West Sussex, 1988).

Another example of organising an enquiry in conceptual terms, this time with an infant class, shows how the complex area of representation can be introduced to young children. This teacher encourages the children to explore the rules and pleasures of stereotyping without the aura of disapproval that this term so often invokes. Yet at the same time she is laying the ground work for more extended work on gender representation, later on.

Investigating a Character Type

We were studying as a school topic the book "The Village Postman" by J and A Ahlberg, which includes reference to several familiar fairy stories. I decided to investigate the stereotyping of princesses in these stories as a media influence on my class of 5 year olds. I knew it would encourage looking at books, developing a visual awareness, plenty of oral discussion thus developing communication skills, close observation and interpreting skills. I wanted them to have the experience of analysing their findings and to define them clearly both in spoken and written forms.

We looked in our book corner and school library for all the books we could find having princesses in the story. We made a display of these and looked closely at the pictures. In a group discussion we decided what a princess should look like. I tape recorded their comments - she would always have yellow or gold hair; her face would always be happy; she would be medium size; she would wear a glittering crown; she would always wear long dresses and have lots of jewellery; she wouldn't wear jeans; she would always be smiling.

I asked them what role did they think a princess has in life - she sits on a throne all day and reads magazines; she would not watch television or do housework; she might talk to visitors to the palace; her servants would cook for her. Their observation of the story books did show there is a stereotyping by the media of princesses in books. Their image of a princess does not yet relate to a real living princess of today.

The children then worked in groups of four looking at ten magazine pictures I had found, the task being to deduce which pictures could be of a princess. (I had included some photographs of our present Royal Princesses). This produced a great deal of discussion and argument as the children had to be critical of the pictures, give opinions and finally agree if this could be a princess or not. Again I tape recorded their comments and wrote them down - black hair isn't right; her shoes are not the right kind; she shouldn't have a bag or wear brown socks; she hasn't got much lipstick; her face is too cross and sad; princesses don't ride bicycles; her eyes are too small, etc. They were able to exhibit close observation of the pictures and their comments show a good imaginative eye to detail.

I finally asked the children to choose one of the pictures which was most like a princess even if in their view it was not a perfect example of one. It was interesting that there was not one universal choice. Six of the pictures were equally popular as the most princess-like person. (A picture of the Queen was eliminated by all the children.) The children wrote their reasons for their choice and even when two children had chosen the same picture, their reasons were often quite different, for example - "I think she is beautiful because she has a long dress and because she has a long necklace"; "I think she is a princess because she has a happy face."

I was impressed with the close observation, discussion and imaginative writing this approach engendered with my very young children. The media do influence their images to a considerable degree. They did have preconceived ideas and as yet their experience excludes close analysis of media techniques, but I do feel this does not mean media education should not be included for this age. It involves many useful process skills and can lead to essential attitudes for learning in the future for these children.

by Christine Goodwin in "Media Education in Primary Schools 2" (occasional papers for teachers of English in West Sussex, Horsham Professional Centre, Clarence Road, Horsham, West Sussex, 1988).

Sometimes it happens that the availability of media technologies (eg a video camera) is the motivation for media education work. It should be noted, however, that media education does not automatically follow from the possession of hardware! Children who are trained or instructed in the "correct" use of technology are learning more about how to take instruction, than they are about the areas of knowledge and understanding that comprise media education - although sometimes this approach is necessitated due to lack of time or confidence. The following accounts show how work that was concentrated on a specific media production opened up media education concepts that suggested further work.

Making a Video

Earlier this year I started a TV topic with my class of third and fourth year juniors in a North London school. The aim was to examine the persuasion techniques for successful commercials.

By chance, someone working on a British Film Institute project visited our school and offered us the loan of a video camera for a couple of weeks. I jumped at the chance to offer the children the equipment to have a go at making their own video. Our headteacher suggested we use the camera to compile a visual school handbook for visitors, parents and governors, and we decided to take up the challenge.

We began by looking at excerpts from different sorts of documentary/documentary style fiction to examine the techniques professionals use to construct their views of the world. We discussed as a class whether we wanted to produce a documentary or an advertisement to "sell" the school; what our viewers would want to see and what aspects of the school we wanted to show. During this preparation time we sent a form around asking staff to tell us when and how they and their children wanted to be filmed.

Learning Process

Our friend from the BFI was only able to spend two days with us, taking us through the basics. She was fairly inexperienced with a camera and I had only managed a couple of hours with the camera and manual myself, so for one or two sessions we worked in groups in a corner of the room or with the whole class, just experimenting and discovering together the things you can do with a camera and microphones. We gave individual children some time simply looking through the camera, handling it and investigating how to focus, monitor light sensitivity, adjust angles, etc. The rest were happy to wait their turn and sat shouting advice. They loved watching themselves appear and disappear on the TV screen we used as a monitor at the front of the classroom.

Ideally, I would have organised them into working groups and let each go through one or two trial runs - erasing and filming over their first efforts - before the "real thing". Lack of time forced me to end this important early learning period.

I grouped the children in fours, trying to keep the timid, younger or less able ones together to avoid them being controlled by more dominant individuals.

Marie Gordon and children at Pakeman School, London, discussing how to video an interview.
Photo: Cary Bazalgette

Team Work

To speed things up I allocated each child a particular role in her "crew" - camera operator, sound controller, director or commentator. The film crews then chose, from the long list we had made, their first filming assignments.

I guided their choice so that the potentially less competent groups took on the subjects that did not require so much organisation and direction, eg interviews with older juniors or adults, small groups of children and less active class lessons.

Next I gave out *storyboard* sheets (draw the frames and lines for writing on, then photocoy them for children to use). The crews used these to make sketches and shooting notes for each shot they planned, frame by frame, indicating where they wanted close-ups, long shots, over-shoulder shots, etc. Particularly for a documentary, the children cannot plan exactly how the shots are going to look, but the process of thinking this through encourages them to make decisions about the position of the camera, what is going to be included in the frame and what will be in the background.

The children were excited and happy to work together co-operatively on their plans. They appreciated that their crew would have only a short time with the equipment and that careful organisation and teamwork were essential as there would be no practice runs. It was now time for children to go around the locations they wanted to film to set up the rooms, plan camera positions, test noise levels, locate power points and rehearse questions they wanted to put to teachers or children.

Work Load

As we discussed and organised the filming it became clear that I would have to be released from teaching the class to take out each film crew and give them my full attention. A supply teacher was brought in to cover for me and cope with the fever of creative activity going on back in the classroom.

This meant that as I started to take crews out on their first assignments around the school, the other children were able to get on with compiling questionnaires for graphs to illustrate favourite school subjects, racial origins of the school's pupils, languages spoken, etc. They prepared captions and drawings, and wrote brief commentaries to go with their pie charts and pictures. Some were busy practising their questioning techniques ready for short interviews with staff or children from other classes about their views on school discipline, homework, the incidence of racism, school councils, etc. The children I worked with found the filming sessions exciting and demanding. Before taking a group out to film, we would look with the previous group at what they had filmed and discuss with them any problems they'd had and any advice they could give.

Making Decisions

The children discovered that they were very much dependent on the others in their crew - for signals, synchronisation of camera and commentary and of movement around the location, for example. They found they were having to make instant decisions - to zoom in close, to raise or lower the sound, cut or extend a shot, ask a follow-up question, and so on.

From the beginning each of them was involved in formulating all the practical steps to produce interesting and attractive images on screen. They were aware that the final product would be the result of their decisions. All of this was a marvellous first-hand learning experience for them - and for me too. They were delighted with the results of their work, as I was despite the frustrations and limitations.

Lessons Learned

In future I would like to give them time to handle the equipment, to just play and try out their ideas. I would want to involve them in any necessary editing of the film. At the Teachers' Centre the room was unfortunately too small to let me take the children in with me. I would also let each child take time to discover the possibilities and problems of filming for herself rather than having me accumulate the skills and pass them on to each new group.

In short, next time I would want to concentrate on helping the children learn from the processes of video-making rather than producing a video film. But this time we just "made a video"!

by Marie Gordon in "Media Education Topic Pack", Junior Education, vol 11 no 11, November 1987

Making a Newspaper

Lurking at the back of my mind was the idea of a class newspaper produced in such a way as to confront at least some of the problems and methods used in the putting together of a local weekly. I've always felt though that news is one of the more problematic areas for 9s and below as they tend not to rate it very highly ... unless, of course, it concerns them, that then seems to be the key to any work in this area at this stage.

The group had worked with with me since September 1985, so we were beginning our second term together, a class of 32 nine year olds, including twelve children attached to the "Warnock Unit" at the school, but who are fully integrated into the class with support coming from the unit staff working alongside me in the classroom for an appropriate number of sessions. The first term had seen a variety of project involving "media" work, from sessions with *Picture Stories* (BFI Education) to work on a five-minute video to sell the Country Code to their peers and younger children, as well as photo stories, conversations, based on pictures of people talking and some storyboarding. All of this work was done in small groups rather than individually.

Just after Christmas the new printer and word processor programme arrived and this seemed an ideal opportunity to try out the newspaper idea. We first looked at, thought about, wrote a few notes on and then talked about the front pages of all the national papers for January 28th 1986, an interesting day since it followed Margaret Thatcher's speech on the Westland affair with headlines varying from the *Mirror's* - "Who Can Trust Her Now" to the *Mail's* "Maggie Stops the Rot", with the *Sun* concentrating more on the fact that Samantha Fox felt "Her boobs were too big". We discussed the headlines, how and why they varied - point of view, truth!, the use of photos and associated captions - how the photo "matched" the story ... why Sam Fox was there ... other front page features ... George Michael's bid to win (in two papers!) ... etc. Generally discussing ideas of audience, serious and trivial treatment ... use of gimmicks etc.

We also looked at a local paper and discussed the differences between that and the national papers, again important ideas about audience - why lots of photos packed with people ... lists of names ... would the main story in the *Melton Times* even make a national paper?

With all this in mind, we had a brainstorming session to produce ideas for our class newspaper to be called the *Sherard Times* (very original! ... their choice). This produced a list of ideas. We appointed, fairly democratically, two editors, a girl and a boy, and then various small groups set to work on the different articles. They arranged interviews, research, photo sessions (they took their own photos on a Canon auto), etc. Once the article was written they checked it out with an editor, and me if they felt the need. It was then typed into the computer by the children and printed out. The particular sample word processor we were using only allowed a one or two column article - because of this we based the A3 size newsheet on five columns. (All my structure imposed beforehand to make it work mechanically).

Headlines were produced from recycled cut out letters and crosswords, cartoons, etc were all produced by the group.

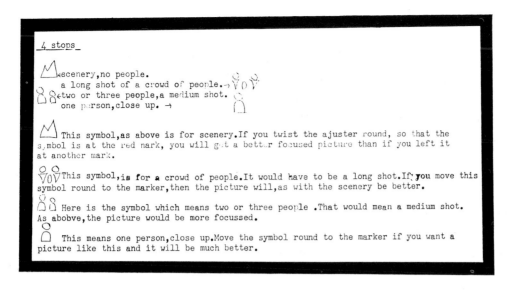

Part of a camera handbook written by 8 and 9 year olds at Brooklands Schoool, London

We began work on Monday, photos were taken to the chemist on Wednesday to be developed by Friday. By this time about half of the paper was pasted up and articles were finished. The editors had control over all layout, choice of main story, etc. Final pasting up and finishing touches were put to the paper on the following Monday, and we (the two editors and myself) took the final eight pages over to the neighbouring High School to photocopy them on their A3 photocopier. We also made A4 copies for each person in the class and others in the school. So within a week - just - and with a great deal of hard work, we produced the *Sherard Times*. Finally we stuck the individual sheets onto a folding backing paper to make it look like an eight page tabloid.

They noticed as we worked on the paper that an obvious missing element was advertising. We had discussed why newspapers carried so much and considered why we had very little and that not paid for. This led to a mad morning of tearing apart the *Daily Mail* with the whole class doing a detailed analysis of the paper expressed as a graph. The class were truly amazed by the high proportion of advertising. Certainly, in another edition, if there is one, the idea of advertising might feature more prominently.

A pleasing, enjoyable week, which I feel took them into and confronted some of the problems of creating a newspaper - and what news is!

"Newspapers" by Paul Merrison in "Working Papers One", BFI Education 1986.

7 | MEDIA EDUCATION AND THE REST OF THE CURRICULUM

We understand that media education may be considered as a cross-curricular theme for ages 5-14 in the National Curriculum. We hope that this will happen, and are encouraged by the English Working Group's recommendations. Although we see media education as particularly closely related to language work, we also see it as permeating the whole curriculum. We would expect teachers with experience and confidence in the media field to be asking "media education questions", and expecting them from children, as a natural part of everyday classroom practice.

Questions such as "Who made this, do you think?" "Why is there a picture on this page?" "How do you think they did that?" "Did your sister enjoy the programme too?" are quite ordinary commonsense questions that teachers and children might be asking anyway, but a consciousness of media education areas of knowledge and understanding will offer the teacher ways of framing questions, and listening to answers, that will open up more possibilities for discussion and investigation.

But this informal "permeation" model of media education does not mean that media education will not figure formally in the curriculum, whether as specifically "media education topics" or as aspects of, or approaches to, other subject areas. The following notes are offered as ways in which work in main subject areas of the curriculum can be consciously enhanced by media education. This does not, of course, simply entail using media in order to teach something else: using, say, a science video uncritically as illustrative or explanatory material would not count as media education. Nor can the argument for media education across the curriculum be reduced to an assertion that it enriches other subjects - though it undoubtedly does. We think that integrating media education with all aspects of the curriculum not only enhances the existing curriculum, but also serves to develop children's critical and creative understandings of the media in a coherent way.

Our suggestions for the ways in which this might be done are necessarily compressed and, in parts, tentative. Further research and development is needed to expand these proposals, to relate them to the appropriate subject working party proposals, and to develop a full account of media education as a cross-curricular theme.

ENGLISH

This section includes the main points of our response to the Cox Committee's report on English for ages 5 to 11 (DES, November 1988).

"Both drama and media studies deal with fundamental questions of language, interpretation and meaning. These seem to us so central to the traditional aims and concerns of English teaching that we would strongly recommend that programmes of study in English should include exploration of both areas." (*English for Ages 5 to 11*, 14.4, p.61)

We agree strongly with this statement, while recognising that the word "include" in the second sentence requires considerable further thought. The programmes of study described in *English for Ages 5 to 11* make minimal reference to the media and virtually none to media education concepts as we have described them. The profile components - Speaking and Listening, Reading, and Writing - relate almost entirely to printed, written and oral forms of language (there is some reference to tape and broadcast forms under Listening); although we note with interest that the Welsh Working Group proposes four profile components: Listening and Watching, Speaking, Reading and Writing (*Interim Report*, 4.9, p.15), and makes reference to "the electronic media" in its statements of attainment.

We have three main responses to make to *English for Ages 5 to 11*, which encompass our proposals for the relationship between media education and English generally. These are:

1. That the profile components, attainment targets and attainment levels in English should be extended to take account of the audio-visual media as study objects within English.

2. That the concepts at present embedded in the statements of attainment and programmes of study be made more explicit, and related to the areas of knowledge and understanding proposed for media education.

3. That further research and development should be planned in order to explore more fully how media education can be integrated with English in programmes of study that will enhance both.

Profile Components and Attainment Targets

We think that these should be extended as follows.

Speaking and Listening should become Speaking, Listening ***and Watching.*** The attainment target in this component should become: "Pupils should demonstrate their understanding of the spoken word and of the audio-visual media, and their capacity to express themselves effectively in a variety of speaking and listening activities, matching style and response to audience and purpose."

Reading Attainment target I: The development of the ability to read, understand and respond to all types of ***text (written, printed and audio-visual).***
Attainment target II: The development of reading and information-retrieval strategies for a ***range of purposes using a variety of media.***

Writing Attainment target I: A growing ability to construct and convey meaning in written *and audio-visual languages.*

Levels of Attainment and Statements of Attainment

The above amendments would result in a number of alterations to the statements of attainment but we feel that a general comment needs to be made about these.

The account of English generally in the report would benefit from a more explicit definition of the *concepts* that children are expected to learn: as we have attempted to do in our account of the areas of knowledge and understanding that media education entails. There is a considerable overlap between our areas and the concepts that are implicit in the attainment targets for English.

The report's emphasis on structure, narrative, grammar and syntax correlates with our concern for media languages. Thus, Level 1 under Reading attainment target I, in demanding that children recognise that print conveys meaning, can be directly connected to our Level 3 attainment target, "Understand that all parts of a media text have meaning and were put there on purpose." The Writing attainment levels which demand an understanding of the function of capital letters, full stops, paragraphs, etc are parallel to our targets for observing, identifying and discussing features such as close up and long shot, sharp and soft focus. Both the Reading and Writing attainment levels could be enhanced by including the concept of *convention* which underlies much language use and forms of writing.

An understanding of convention relates fruitfully to the way categories are conceptualised, and this is also an area common to both *English for Ages 5 to 11* and our curriculum statement. A number of attainment levels in the former expect children to understand appropriate contexts for the use of Standard English, or for different layouts of text; to distinguish between kinds of narrative; to use classification systems. We think these could be extended to include understandings of the *reasons* for category differences: historical, technological, social, institutional, etc. This is touched on in 10.33, but it could be further developed.

Our other three areas of knowledge and understanding are represented in the Programmes of Study, but we think English could benefit markedly from their being made more explicit in the statements of attainment. Nothing in these asks children to develop a sense of authorship: that texts are made by people; that different books by the same person may have similarities; that a writer living in a different time or place may write differently from someone living here and now. These are traditional, literary understandings, and we are surprised not to find them in the report. Extended to our more general notion of *agency*, we think it would be useful for children to be investigating who gets into print, and how, and how books get made and published, just as we would expect them to acquire similar understanding about audio-visual texts.

A sense of *audience* is also only implicit in the statements of attainment. To whom do children read aloud and why? For whom do they write? For what purposes is impersonal writing required? We think that our attainment targets under this heading - for example understanding that the decision to address a particular audience will affect what goes into a text and how it is presented and circulated - are essential prerequisites that enable children to develop an understanding of what *is* "appropriate", "well-structured" and "logical". This is well set out in 10.33 in terms of classroom practice, but we would like to see it as an explicit learning goal.

There is little in *English for Ages 5 to 11* on what texts are about. Texts in any medium have a relation to reality: this is hinted at elliptically in the report when "non chronological writing" or "fiction and non-fiction" are cited. Children are interested in whether and why, and to what extent, a text is "true" or not. They are upset by frightening or offensive material - in print just as on television. We think that English should explicitly deal with the concept of *representation* in order to explore these questions, and to lead into investigation of how social groups, events and ideas are represented in all kinds of text.

We also wish to comment more extensively on the report's account of literature (pp 27-29) and the implications this has for the statements of attainment. We agree wholeheartedly that children should have "as great an experience as possible of the best imaginative literature". But we note that little consideration is given in chapter 6 to the fact that children's experience of narrative, of "more lives than their own" (6.2), of "the ideas and feelings of people from cultures different from their own" (6.3), of "new forms of expression and modes of discourse" (6.4), of "rhythm, pattern and rhyme" (6.5) and of "the presence of literary references" (6.6) does not come only from literature. Television, cinema, comics and radio also all contribute, in their own ways, to the development of these kinds of knowledge and understanding, as do literary forms that do not usually get classed as "the best imaginative literature". Children enter school at five with an already extensive understanding of fictional narrative and audio-visual languages (just how extensive, we need more research to discover). Some of their media experience (television story-telling and serialisation of classic children's novels, for instance) relates very closely to, and encourages interest in, the "good literature" cited in *English for Ages 5 to 11*. We think that English teaching in the primary school should acknowledge this experience and build upon it. Just as it seeks to extend and diversify children's literary experience, it should also be introducing them to a broader range of audio-visual texts: independent film, video art or radio drama, for example. These have a valid contribution to make in enriching children's language experience and "allow the individual greater possibilities of *production* of language" (*Kingman Report*, 2.23, quoted in *English for Ages 5 to 11*, 6.4, p.27).

Stacey Walker, aged 6, drawing and writing about Fireman Sam at Sherard School, Leics. Photo: Paul Merrison

Thus, many of the statements of attainment listed under Reading attainment target I, such as "say what has happened and what may happen in stories" (Level 2), or "make some use of inference, deduction and reading experience to reach meanings which are beyond the literal" (Level 3), or "show developing tastes and preferences over an increased range of material" (Level 5) can all be developed through systematic critical study of audio-visual texts as well as written or printed ones. Likewise, under Reading Attainment target II, the emphasis on the use of information books and printed signs is remarkable given the fact that adults get enormous amounts of information from the press, magazines, television news and documentary, teletext, training videos, instructional tape, disc and computer programmes. The ability "to evaluate information sources and critically to weigh evidence and argument" must surely take all of these into account.

The levels of attainment in Writing should, we feel, take a fuller account of the kinds of writing that media education entails. Some of these are already present: listing (Level 2), revision and redrafting (Level 3), using layout (Level 4). But others could also be included, such as writing, argument, description or narrative from different points of view, for different audiences, for different purposes and in a variety of formats. The combination of pictures and writing, as in captioning, illustrating or storyboarding, could also be included.

In addition, the Writing attainment levels include activities that can relate to forms of production other than the written: "Structure sequences of real or imagined events coherently in chronological accounts" (Level 2), and "produce well-structured narratives with an opening, a setting, characters, a series of events and a resolution" (Level 4). These can be developed through audio-visual production as well as through writing, and our experience suggests that the inclusion of audio-visual production work enhances children's understanding of textual structures and their motivation to write.

Programmes of Study

There are a few points in the Programmes of Study where media education activities are touched upon: writing in response to television programmes (10.30, p.52); creating a class newspaper (10.33, p.52); many of the activities listed under Speaking and Listening (8.23, 8.24, p.37); reading newspapers (9.13, p.44). We think such references could be far more extensive.

The Speaking and Listening activities should include the use of audio and video tape as a way of enhancing almost all of the listed activities, as well as developing understanding of these media. Many speaking and listening activities can themselves relate closely to the media and help develop media understanding: reading a news bulletin; conducting an interview; chairing and participating in discussion; improvising, or writing and reading aloud, a commentary on a live or recorded event. Any close analysis of audio-visual texts entails careful listening to speech and sound and discussing their meaning. It can also involve judging how words and sounds affect the meaning of images, and vice versa.

The range of reading materials cited in 9.13 should include titles, credits, logos, headlines, captions, packaging details, comic strip "bubbles", radio and TV schedules and scripts. But, reading should encompass the study of audio-visual texts. Programmes of study should therefore include viewing films (both in school and in the cinema), television programmes and videos; listening to radio and to audio tape, and reading newspapers and magazines. All these should take place in the context of critical questioning and discussion.

The writing assignments cited in 10.33 should include scripting for film, video and sound tape as well as play scripts; note taking; newspaper reporting; editing and cutting to required time lengths; writing headlines and sub-heads; writing letters to public bodies such as television companies or newspaper editors. Additionally, "writing" should be extended to all forms of audio-visual production.

More detailed accounts of media teaching approaches are given in section 6 of our curriculum statement (see above, p.28).

Finally, we would like to comment on the section of the report entitled "The Role of English in the Curriculum". Paragraph 3.24 here implies that media education is to be found in the "cultural analysis" view of English and 3.26 implies that this is more relevant to the later years of compulsory schooling.

We believe that a smiliar range of views applies to media education. A "personal growth" view for example would respect the child's own media experience and values, along with her native language or dialect. A "cross curricular" view recognises that, like English, the media can be both a subject and a medium of instruction for other subjects. An "adult needs" view recognises the citizen's need for a high standard of critical media literacy. A "cultural heritage" view emphasises the responsibility of schools to ensure that children experience the films and broadcast drama that have been significant in our cultural history. We thus see media education as appropriate from the earliest years of schooling. We also see it as more closely related to English than to any other subject area, although, as will become clear in the following sections, we do not by any means see it as confined to English.

SCIENCE

"Science is a continuous process by which individuals and groups develop an understanding of the physical and biological aspects of the world. It is a way in which reliable knowledge about the world is progressively established through the generation and testing of ideas and theories". (*Science for ages 5 to 16*, 2.2, p.6). Given the scientific goals of developing a true understanding and reliable knowledge about the world, there is a natural tendency to condemn many representations of science in the media as necessarily wrong or inaccurate. But the media are a major source of children's ideas about science, scientists and what is scientific, and they usually generate an excitement about science which, even when it is misdirected or inappropriate, is still a potential motivation and needs open consideration and negotiation rather than rejection.

Science and Media Education

Media technologies are based on a range of scientific principles which are worth investigating for their own sake, but which additionally enhance children's understanding of the media and in particular their sense of the creative potential of different technologies. A firm link between creative arts and science can thus be established, which will be of benefit to both. Some of these principles are:

- **printing:** reverse images, symmetry, positive and negative images, using potatoes, lino, screen printing, photocopying and computer printouts. The latter two can also be used to investigate changes in scale.

- **photography:** experiments with light-sensitive materials and developing chemicals, lenses, focusing and reflection of light, also using pinhole cameras, viewfinders and a range of different camera types.

- **radio:** experiments with vibration and diaphragms, using balloons, string telephones and simple radio kits.

- **film:** both film and television are based on the principle of persistence of vision, exploration of which is supported by a wide range of published material. Projection can be explored using lenses, slide projector or an OHP, and examining slides or strips of film.

- **electronic media:** it is harder to investigate the basic principles of television, video and computers, but ample opportunities exist in schools for exploring the capabilities of these technologies.

9 year old at Oundle Primary School, Northants

Science in the media

Children can explore, investigate or research the ways that "science" is presented in *all* media forms, not just factual and documentary. For example

- *comics:* science fiction, scientists, and the breaking of scientific principles such as gravity, eg by superhero figures

- *newspapers:* what kinds of science are reported regularly, what kinds occasionally; how this varies in different papers

- *cinema:* how science is used, reported and explored, especially in fiction films such as science fictions, space fantasy thrillers; the relation between science and magic

- *television:* how science features on TV; similarities and differences across a range of programmes, eg from *Tomorrow's World* to *Dr Who* and including the weather forecast, *The Sky at Night* as well as schools programmes and nature documentaries. What is shown, how, when and for whom.

Some of the recurrent themes - the scientist, "rule-breaking" etc - could be explored *across* a range of media forms.

Global problems such as the ozone layer, acid rain, deforestation, etc need consideration in terms of the part the media play in informing us - and not informing us.

MATHEMATICS

Media education requires mathematical knowledge and skills in many of its activities. Developing mathematical work within a media education context is also likely to promote understanding of mathematical concepts, and children's motivation in handling them. The following notes indicate a range of activities.

Mathematics and media education

- *Survey:* investigating the popularity of TV programmes, newspapers, comics, records, etc amongst a given group; counting numbers in various categories; presenting results in block graph or pie chart form.

- *Percentages:* making direct comparisons, eg percentage of different newspapers devoted to particular features.

- *Time:* investigating length of programmes, films and advertisements; analysing TV and radio schedules; timing sections of programmes; planning video, film or sound tape productions and timing sections to exact length; manipulating or calculating small sections of time, eg short lengths, shutter speeds in cameras.

- *Number calculations:* changes in focal length, tape speed, frames per second, and the effects these have.

- *Measurement:* planning or analysing page layouts in posters, newspapers, books, etc; relating time measurements to physical measurements (eg of film); measuring camera or microphone distances, projector throw; framing and cropping.

Victoria Wilson, aged 6, finishing a graph of programmes watched on one day. Sherard School, Leics. Photo: Paul Merrison

Mathematics in the media

The following aspects of media output can be noted and explored in terms of mathematical concepts:
- Use of numbers, percentages, graphs and charts in the presentation of news, sport, advertising, weather, documentaries etc.

- Use of surveys and polls, circulation and viewing figures.

- Use of comparative language to increase excitement or persuasive effect.

- How different kinds of framing, camera angles, camera movement and zooms are used to include/exclude parts of what is being shown.

- Uses of scoring systems and time limits in sport, game shows and quizzes.

- Uses of special effects to alter scale, perspective, perceptions of time and space.

- Costs of production, advertising space, etc.

- Use of numbers and dates to imply credibility, status, novelty, etc.

HISTORY

"How do you know" is a key question in media education, and in history. History is concerned with evidence, and with investigating the nature of evidence. Much historical evidence can be seen as media texts: documents, pictures, inscriptions, books; as well as photographs, films and recorded material from the more recent past. Arguments can be made for other kinds of historical evidence, such as buildings or clothing, as being media texts also, expressing power and status to their contemporaries. But the media also feature *in* history: part of understanding an historical period is to do with understanding how information and entertainment were circulated in society and who had the power to control systems of communication.

History and media education

- *Looking at time:* egg timers, clocks, stop watches, calendars, diaries.

- *Looking at "yesterday":* TV schedules, TV programmes watched, newspapers, letters received, own news.

- *Looking at News items:* look at the ways in which, eg Royalty is reported on and discuss why these matters are reported and take the form they do.

- *Considering traditions and festivals:* their roots and how they are represented in the media currently.

- *Bringing historical artefacts into school:* discuss and research them.

- *Examining historical buildings and/or artefacts:* consider the messages these convey about use and life style.

- *Talking to older people:* record on audio or video tape and ask about their experiences or about specific topics, eg World War II. Retain these interviews as source material. Check differences between this data and that available through other media sources.

- *Exploring history through drama:* script, rehearse, perform dramatic pieces on famous historical events. Record results in various ways - photograph them, video them, paint them, write about them. Research the whole matter through consulting various media sources, develop a critical concern for evidence.

- *Constructing historical graphs:* local events, national events, international events.

History in the media

- Research in local library for *photographs* of local area, buildings, interiors and exteriors, as evidence of another life style in terms of work, clothes, shopping - compare to existing situation. Discuss and research why these changes occurred.

- Look at/listen to *factual programmes on TV and radio,* especially those that relate to the recent past. Ask children to research these at home with older members of the family. Speculate on reasons for change occurring.

- Look at recent historical examples of *art and music* and identify differences and speculate on causes, eg changes in work or ideas; advances in technology.

- Look at *fictional historical drama,* at examples of social control and conflict, at interdependence and co-operation and identify important features - power, life style, women's role, customs, languages and clothes, and research the accuracy of these.

- Look at *how jobs are represented* in various media - old paintings, literature, film, etc and make deductions about other consequent features of life.

- Look at *media productions* generally and look at the way historical periods, figures, and "the past" generally are represented, and at when and why stereotyping occurs.

- Look at *how the media foresee the future* - space fantasy, programmes such as *Tomorrow's World.* Speculate on their accuracy. Look at examples from the past, eg H.G. Wells' predictions.

- Make judgements about the *authenticity* of historical media evidence, eg engravings of scenes in 19th century newspapers; ballads about contemporary people and events.

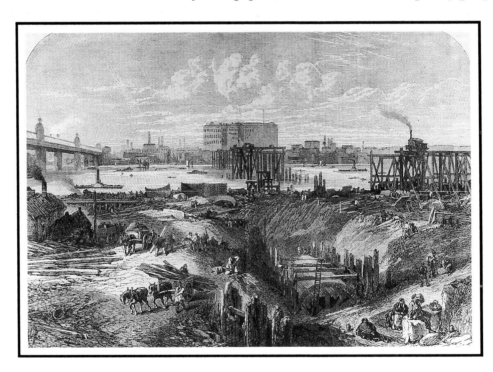

*Illustrated Times
August 17th
1867: The Works
at Whitehall, of
the pneumatic
railway from
Charing Cross to
Waterloo Station.*

GEOGRAPHY

People in Western society now have a clearer sense of what other parts of their own country and of the rest of the world are like, than at any other time in history. This is due to the fact that the media constantly present us with images of different parts of the world, whether in news, drama, documentary, travel brochures, famine relief appeals or advertising. This is not to say that these representations are accurate or complete, or that they are all of equal status. Media education encourages children to explore the nature of the representations they can make of their own localities and of places they visit, and the status and comprehensiveness of the representations they see in the media.

Geography and media education

- *Photography and other images:* take photographs of the local area in terms of - local features; of terrain and environment (rural, urban); housing; climate; availability and form of food; animal life; employment. Make a poster/picture/video of local area as above.

- *Scale:* look at the enlargement and reduction possibilities of photocopiers.

- *Maps:* make maps of birds-eye view of everyday objects, school room, street, route to school, with attention to scale as appropriate.

- *Record:* findings in geography work generally in a variety of media, where possible for real audiences.

- *Read, watch, listen to:* factual geographic material in the media and discuss in terms of effects on life style, appearance, eg skin colour, food and employment.

- *Investigating representations:* look at how geographic ideas may be implicitly formed through media links and representations, eg mail delivery (stamps), food packaging (advertising, images of farms and the country), popular music (styles of music, videos, the charitable aspects, eg responses to drought - causes and consequences).

Geography in the media

- Look at existing *photographs* of local area - snapshot, aerial pictures, promotional material and compare to reality, discuss differences, why they exist if they do.

- Look at *photos and other pictorial* images of exteriors and interiors; compare and discuss. Compare with own experiences.

- Look at *tourist advertisements, posters, postcards* - what messages do they convey, why, what can we deduce about particular countries or environments, what can we deduce about particular countries or environments, what can we deduce about how people live and work. Compare this with information from other media materials. Discuss aspects of how terrain, climate and environment dictate life style, food, clothing, housing, employment, music, folk tales, art.

- Look at *TV programmes and advertisements* to see how information about different countries and environments is depicted; consider when and why stereotyping occurs.

- Watch and listen to *fictional TV and radio programmes* that have a regional setting and discuss the constraints and interests these locations dictate, eg *The Archers, Brookside, East Enders.*

- Read, watch, listen to and discuss relevant *educational material* which may include prime time TV natural history programmmes, as well as books, posters, etc.

- Look at *food packaging* and the messages it contains about places of origin.

- Examine *weather forecasts:* what is considered important information, and what isn't and why.

- Examine other *visual symbols* relating to the environment such as road signs, maps, atlases, lighthouses, etc.

ART

Like language work, art is so closely related to media education that opportunities for integrating the two have no doubt been obvious throughout this document. It is worth stressing again, however, that our view of media education emphasises creative production, and that children must wherever possible have the opportunity to explore the uses of media technologies imaginatively, and not be confined to using them as recording devices. Children's media production work will obviously involve art work at all stages: storyboarding, design of titles and credits, making figures and models for animation, devising advertisements, whether in film, video or poster form, making masks, disguises and costumes for film or video drama, and so on. It is thus impossible to produce an exhaustive list of media education activities in art. The following indicates broad areas.

Art and Media Education

- *Design and graphics:* designing and making titles, title pages, book covers, record sleeves, general packaging, logos.

- *Planning and drafting* storyboards, camera movements, framing of an image, masking off different parts of an image, trying out different captions, commentaries or music.

- Exploring *pattern and repetition* in animation, collage using photographs from magazines, photographs and tape-slide of patterns in the environment.

- *Three-dimensional work:* making models for sets, figures for animation, masks.

- Exploring a visual idea in *different media,* eg photos for storyboard transformed into comic strip, then animated sequence, then dramatised.

- Exploring *media technologies* creatively: painting, drawing or scratching on film, drawing around still or projected image or shadow, projecting drawings on an OHP; shadow puppets, computer graphics, lighting effects, using photographic or video "mistakes" in imaginative ways.

Art in the media

Media education offers new ways of looking at and thinking about artistic production: painting and sculpture can be considered as media texts and "media education questions" asked about them. But all media can be considered as art forms, having just as much potential for creative expression as traditional forms.

Questions about how a scene is framed - even a news interview or an advertisement - involve aesthetic issues just as much as informational ones. From this broad range of possibilities, we indicate here just a few ways in which art and design in the media might be considered.

-   ***Print:*** look at differences in style and purpose of illustrations, and diferent media used; design of books, covers and title pages; posters, stamps, informational material, magazines and newspapers: how all these differ across cultures and over time.

-   ***Film and Television*** title sequences and credits and how these relate to the programmes; company logos and trailers; quiz shows, sports programmes, news, etc.

-   ***Drama*** in film and television: the composition of images, use of colour, costume and set esign. This can be done most effectively using stills or frame slides.

Conifer sprays: developer picture by 7 year olds at Hollinswood First School, Shropshire. The sprays were placed on photographic paper in safe lighting, then developed and processed, by the children, in the usual way

MUSIC

There are clearly many ways in which music education can be enhanced through work with media, as well as being a vital contribution to media education. This is true of all the aspects of music: composing, performing and listening.

Music and Media Education

- *Composing* music and sound effects to accompany video, film and slide projection. Exploring the effect of using different instruments and different combinations of sounds with the same images. Investigating different ways of using microphones to amplify and distort sounds. Exploring the effect of silence in relation to particular images or sequences.

- *Listening* to pre-recorded music and sound effects and trying these out in different ways to accompany images. Listening to music and sound effects, then devising and making images to accompany them. Using music in radio, drama and other sound tape forms.

- *Performing* on different instruments and making sound effects with a variety of materials, to accompany visual images. Working out ways of achieving particular sound or musical effects. Singing and chanting accompaniments to visual material.

10 year old children at Sherard School, Leics, dubbing their own music onto a 60 second video developed in response to a photograph. Photo: Paul Merrison

Music in the media

This is of course a vast area: an essential aspect of studying almost any audio-visual text involves thinking about the music and sound effects and how these contribute to the meaning. These are just a few of the possibilities.

-   music in *film and televison:* in music shows, pop videos and programmes about music and musicians, as well as title sequence music, background music etc. Listen to music without visuals, watch visuals without music, and discuss the effects; try different music with a particular sequence; analyse how scenes are cut to music; how music is used for emotional effects and suspense.

-   music on *radio:* what's available, and what isn't; how you find out what's on when; how music is used in drama; who listens to what.

-   the *music industry:* how records are promoted and distributed; how different groups and styles are promoted; film and television promotion through music; how the music industry has developed over time; how people heard and found out about music before recording was invented.

DRAMA

There is an obvious sense in which drama connects with media work, in the recording of drama exercises or performances. But in this context the medium used - whether sound tape, video, photography or film - is usually seen as a way of preserving performances, rather than as a way of transforming them. At the very least, such a process ought to give rise to questions like "What difference will video make to the performance? What can we show with video that a live performance can't show - and what can't video show?" Video and sound tape can contribute to drama methods, adding a new dimension to the processes through which children "can gain understanding of themselves and others, can gain confidence in themselves as decision-makers and problem-solvers, can learn to function collaboratively" (*English for Ages 5 to 11,* 14.7, p.62)

Media education activities within drama need not involve media technologies at all, however. We list some possibilities below.

Drama and Media Education

-   *Simulation*-type exercises or improvisations that explore roles such as publisher, TV producer, film crew etc, integrate drama with media education and can be one of the best ways of considering this area.

-   *Interviewing, presenting, newsreading* and *commentating* all offer ways of understanding the authoritative voices of the media as well as developing children's own confidence and articulacy. Often the "media" context of recording such activities is itself confidence-building.

-   *Reporting* actual research and investigation back to the rest of the class in the style of different forms or genres: documentary, news, travelogue, weather report, or *Blue Peter* style instruction.

-   *Dramatising* a well-known story in a different generic style, eg "The Three Little Pigs" as a crime thriller. Exploring the different styles of media forms: reportage, soap opera, game shows, etc.

Drama in the media

Apart from the obvious consideration of dramatic performance in the media, a number of drama exercises relating to media content can be envisaged.

- Taking a visual image such as an advertisement, a photograph or painting and improvising the events leading up to that moment, or following on from it - or both.

- Exploring the limits of particular media conventions such as the "rules" governing who can look at the camera and who can't.

- Trying out film/video effects in real life, moving in slow motion, fast forward, action replay or freeze frame.

- Taking on the role of an animal character from comics or cartoons.

- Using speech bubble dialogue from comics as a script.

HEALTH EDUCATION AND P. E.

Children get many of their ideas about health and illness from the media, and sport is one of the most popular television forms. So teaching in both these areas will benefit from an active, critical consideration of the media, rather than ignoring them, using them illustratively, or teaching "against" them.

PE, Health Education and Media Education

- *Audio taped commentaries* to accompany a series of illustrations, eg about breathing, circulation, or digestion; or about school PE or sport activities.

- Make *flip books* or *zoetropes* showing body movements. Show the working of the body (cells etc) through animation.

- *Advertising:* look at advertisements in magazines, newspapers, and on television. How they try to get us interested in foods, how many brands there are of the same thing, and how they compare.

- *Packaging*: investigating the difference between the presentation of packaging of "junk food" and "wholesome" food.

- *Music:* look at how music is used on television and radio to create mood and affect emotions. Exploring how music can be used to accompany different movements in sport.

- Make a *video* to convey information about healthy eating, invasion of germs, visiting the doctor, dentist, the school nurse, etc; or about PE or sport.

- Try to *record* a school sporting activity through writing, photography, sound tape or video - or combinations of all these. What are the difficulties? How are they best overcome given the available technology?

Health issues in the media

Look at health care articles in magazines and specialist journals. What are they about? Is there a particular preoccupation with any one issue? Comment on health programmes on radio and television. Look at health warnings, eg smoking, preservatives, food additives.

P.E. and Sport in the Media

Given that P.E. and games help prepare children for the world of adult sport and recreation, and that the media show professional sport at its best and at its worst, teachers can help children to explore their perceptions of sport and sportspeople, by considering media sports coverage.

- Consider the prominence or otherwise of sport in the news.

- Consider representation in the news of women, men and children who are involved in sporting activities, investigate who gets represented and who doesn't; what sports are "newsworthy"; how newspaper, *TV* and *Radio Times* coverage of sports events encourage us to take an interest in particular sports; what is shown when, and why.

- Consider the coverage of sport on TV, radio and in the Press; investigate how much coverage there is, in terms of time or page area; whether sports programmes are a separate category ie, are they all alike, and different from other forms.

- Discuss how a "new" sport could be promoted through the media (eg hopscotch, tiddlywinks).

DESIGN and TECHNOLOGY

"Communication, in its broadest sense, involving not only talking, listening, reading and writing, but graphical representation, modelling, model making, and other ways of representing mental images, is of vital importance to design and technological capability ... because most design and technological activity in the world of work involves collaboration in a team, it requires the exercise of skills of negotiating with others; persuading; understanding the points of view of others; criticising and accepting criticism; and accepting compromise." (Design and Technology Working Group Interim Report, DES November 1988, 1.35, p.14).

"It is a matter for schools how they might bring together the diverse areas of knowledge, skills, understanding and values necessary for decision-making and problem-solving in the area of design and technology." (*ibid* 1.36, p.15).

We agree with the Working Group that "design and technology in the curriculum of primary and secondary schools is inescapably integrative in its nature and will require contributions from a variety of curriculum sources" (*ibid*). We would in fact argue that *all* subject areas have, or should have, a design and technology component. As far as media education is concerned, we believe that the attainment targets we cite under Media Technology (see above, p.24) would constitute a useful addition to the attainment targets listed by the Working Group.

10 year olds at Sherard School building models for their video. Photo: Paul Merrison

There is a real sense in which the profile components and attainment targets as described in the Working Group's Interim Report can be seen as an integral part of media education. They do not, of course, by themselves constitute media education, but when seen in this context acquire a critical and analytical dimension that seems to us essential if children's motivation and commitment to design and technology is to be maintained. We list below some notes on design and technology activities which are part of media education.

- *Awareness of energy:* bulbs and batteries in the camera and tape recorder. Working with and alongside technical equipment: video, tape recorder, camera, projector and computers.

- *Structures:* constructing sets, models and frame works, eg box camera, pretend TV set. Using a variety of woods, surfaces and materials, altering the surfaces to suit the purpose and design of the project.

- *Using tools* to cut, shape, hold, join and glue models and sets for communication, animation and video productions.

- *Controlling parts of machinery* such as rollers, cranks, cogs.

- Learning how to *communicate in a visual medium.* Understanding the elements of design. Problem solving and working co-operatively on a common project.

- *Lighting control:* changing for colour, atmosphere and illumination.

- *Newspapers:* layout design, size and shape.

- *Models* for communication projects; designing non-verbal messages, such as traffic lights.

- *Paper engineering;* levers for body joints in an animation model, vehicles, puppets and special effects.

- *Observation and discussion* of design and technology features in the media themselves, such as structures found on film and television sets; trolleys, tripods, dolly, cranes. Models, puppets, jointed figures.
  Control mechanism: rollers, cogs, cranks, sprocket holes, winding mechanisms, presses, gears, wheels, spindles.
  Awareness of design, eg shapes fitting inside shapes (cassette, film and tape); graphics, sets, lighting.
  Exploring how special effects and stunts are achieved.

INFORMATION TECHNOLOGY

"Information Technology ... [has] to do with the storage, retrieval, processing and transmission of 'information'" (*English for ages 5 to 11,* 14.15, p62) It has little to do with the creation or interpretation of the "information" it deals with. "Information" in this sense is analogous to the "signal" which passes from TV transmitter to TV screen, although the signal may be stored on video tape before receipt. "Information theory" is a specialised and rapidly developing mathematical discipline, and the subject of Information Technology (I.T.) developed by and from it has tended to be highly skills-based, teaching how to handle keyboards and to programme computers.

The English Working Group's comments are encouraging, but could be extended. Information technologies are, after all, media, and the same questions can be asked about them as of any other media. Our proposed attainment targets suggest that at attainment level 3 children should "be able to identify simple technological differences between and within media", and should "understand that technological choices make a difference to the meaning of a text". Media education should thus develop children's critical understanding of information technology.

Information Technology in Media Education

- What differences *word processing and desktop publishing* programmes make to the appearance, and hence the apparent status, of written work.

- Devising and writing a *computer game* for friends or children in another class or age group.

- Exploring *typography and layout* for the production of newspaper or magazine pages, and editing text to fit a particular format.

- using *design, paint and graphics* programmes to devise logos, and credit sequences, and patterns for abstract animation.

Information Technology and the media

- view and discuss the use of *computers* in films and television: when is their use plausible, and when does it simply stand in for "magic"?

- compare computer animation and graphics with other graphic and animated forms; consider what the differences are and what the one can do that others can't.

- investigate computerised mailing lists by examining junk mail; find out how you get on to a list - and how you get off it; how - and why - letters are "personalised".

Emma Hockridge and Maria Rowe, aged 8, using Logo Script word processor to produce an article for their paper Wildlife News. Copplestone School, Devon. Photo: Sandra Sutton

RELIGIOUS EDUCATION

Many agreed religious education syllabuses are likely to contain the following four main elements:

- the acquisition of knowledge about religion
- the exploration of and reflection on human experience
- the learning of necessary skills
- the development of sensitive attitudes.

In each of these areas media education provides opportunities for enrichment and enhancement of insight. Many of the popular television programmes watched by children and feature films available for hire from video libraries are of an allegorical nature. This material is part of the common experience of most pupils, and teachers alive to the possibilities can make much use of it.

The Primary Working Party found that moral distinctions between characters in stories were an important preoccupation for young children in particular (eg "goodies" and "baddies"); we consider that religious education could build on this concern and encourage children to discuss how moral qualities are represented in characters' appearance and how they are played out in the narrative. Most narratives deal with moral dilemmas and the exploration of these can be central to religious education.

It is also possible to see religions themselves as media: as systems for communication and social cohesion. The stories of religious innovators and leaders such as Jesus can be examined in terms of how they transformed contemporary religious ideas, and how the new ideas were spread to large numbers of people (see also History section above, p.65).

Children can also examine the ways in which religion features in the media. How many religious programmes are there on radio and television? What religions are featured most? How often are actual religious services broadcast, and when? Why are they broadcast? Do the media observe non-Christian festivals in any ways? How are non-Christian religions represented in travel and documentary programmes?

Stephen, aged 8,
Drayton Park
School, London

I think this boy is helping his sister because she went to the shop for a doll. For the dolls house. His sister came back and saw him and she took a photograph of him. Afterwards she showed it to him and he said,"I will get you" he slad I think he slad I will get you. because it's unusual for a boy. To play with a dolls house

EQUAL OPPORTUNITIES: Race, Gender and Class

Equal opportunities policies seek to ensure that all social and ethnic groups in the school feel that they are a valued part of the school community and have a contribution to make. Media education has a vital contribution to make to both of these areas. It is through the media that children gain a great deal of information about different social groups and different parts of the world. They also gain a sense of what is regarded as "normal" and "ordinary" in our culture. Some of these messages are valuable and extend children's sense of a world community; some of them are misleading and partial; some of them are malignant. Media education helps children to assess media representations of groups and places, to criticise them constructively, and to imagine how they might be different. This is better than censoring, excluding or simply condemning certain representations.

Equal Opportunities and Media Education

- An activity for younger infant children: ***planning and taking a photograph*** of your family (camera loaned from school).

  These photos would vary, show different forms of dress from jeans to saris, different sizes of family from single parent with one child to large extended families; families that include someone who is handicapped; very old/young families; families with pets; different hairstyles.

  The children would have to choose the background of their photo, the kitchen, the front room, the yard or garden, by the car, on the balcony and so on, and then explain why they chose that background.

- An activity for older primary children could be to ***look at the photographs/images*** used to promote fashion and beauty products in advertising.

  First collecting examples, then looking at what kind of models are used to sell what - young/old; European/African/Asian; pretty/ugly; working class/middle class; rich/poor. What kind of homes are shown? In what magazines do black glamour models appear? What kind of clothes do women wear when advertising makeup and other beauty products?

- Again with older primary children, ***content analyses*** can be undertaken, and percentage graphs produced, to analyse the representation of third world countries in the media in terms of positive and negative images; this depends on careful consideration of what "positive" and "negative" might mean, in context.

Cultural and Social Representations in the Media

- Examining how contemporary Britain and the rest of the world are represented in and by the media, recognising the enormous influence that the media play in influencing our views and beliefs. This involves looking at newspapers, magazines, comics, books (including text books), radio, all types of TV (popular, news, documentary, schools TV), video, cinema, advertising.

- Looking at the representations of social class, age, children, old people, different ethnic groups, locations in the world, Europe, America, developing countries, religions, food, clothes, customs, men and women.

  Identifying who in our society is under-represented or indeed invisible in certain sections of the media (eg, images of the disabled are rarely used in adversting).

- Doing surveys, polls, gathering and sorting information, comparing images, comparing interpretations, considering different points of view, bias, and circulation to different audiences.

8 PEDAGOGY

Many teachers believe that media education must entail good primary practice: respecting children's knowledge, points of view and creativity; exploring with them aspects of the world that are interesting and relevant to them; encouraging group collaboration, discussion, questioning, creative and investigative work, and so on. We do however want to make some remarks about pedagogy, arising from points of difficulty that are sometimes raised by teachers.

Explicit and Implicit Aims

Media education can sometimes provoke an anxiety about how the children percieve the value and purpose of what they are doing. Investigating a current media "craze" such as a popular TV programme or the latest vogue in sticker collections, may seem like an unwarranted intrusion into children's private lives, or into an area they have already identified for themselves as an idle pastime: something you do in order to relax *after* school, not something you have to think about *in* school. Even if this doesn't happen, teachers may feel that by valuing children's enthusiasms, what they are really doing is letting television companies or sticker manufacturers set the agenda for what is discussed in the classroom. Detailed study of an advertisement can result in the children celebrating the skills of the producers and being even more keen on the product.

But if the aims of media education are to teach particular skills, knowledge and understanding, then any text that helps to do this can be used. Media education can never be regarded as a way of changing children's own media preferences to bring them in line with what the teacher - or indeed the Secretary of State - approves of. But it can be regarded as a way of encourgaing children to analyse their preferences critically and, if appropriate, to challenge them or to argue for them.

Although an important premise of media education is that popular entertainment forms are worthy of serious attention, it would be failing children if it dealt only with such forms. Children should have opportunities of encountering independent, alternative and experimental media texts, and should be able to explore the creative potential of the media in their own productions.

Learning Through Doing

It is sometimes claimed that children are "bound" to learn about the media through their own media production. Sometimes this claim is a very literal one: children learn about television by making television programmes. But in fact children practically never make *television*: they make videos, which is a different form, just as writing stories in the classroom doesn't necessarily teach you much about the publication of novels. Neither would children's imaginative use of the media necessarily be fostered by imitating the work of major producers. But even when this disclaimer is acknowledged, problems still remain.

There is a lot more we need to know about what children are learning, conceptually, through practical media work. Are children the active media communicators they are often claimed to be? Do children find things to photograph, film or video "just popping up"? If they do, are they allowed to pursue this, and how does this connect with the critical understanding we want them to develop? Do such approaches support an investigative approach to the media or do they involve children in trying to reproduce dominant media forms?

These are all questions we have asked ourselves in the Working Party and have no cut-and-dried answers to them. We acknowledge them as possible problems in any primary practices, and worth using as a basis for constructive criticism of our own and each other's work.

Two areas that seem crucial to much good media education practice are collaborative work and discussion. Both of these can be difficult to handle in primary classrooms. We are indebted to Ian Sandbrook who prepared the following comments on these aspects of pedagogy as notes towards a framework for primary media education, in ILEA.

Sharon Forby, Chris Broad, Tom Eason, Kelly Smith and Ruth Measures (all aged 10) working on a musical score for their video. Sherard School, Leics.
Photo: Paul Merrison

Collaboration

Investigating and creating media products lends itself particularly well to collaborative activity. (This is not to say that media education work cannot be done by individuals). However, successful group work, where children do more than work as individuals side by side, is notoriously difficult to organise.

Collaboration is seen as a specific aspect of achievement in *Improving Primary Schools* (the "Thomas Report"), which has to be taught and learned. Collaboration is important because the thinking power of a whole group is greater than the sum of its parts. People working together skillfully can combine their experience, knowledge and intellects to think new thoughts. Beyond this there are skills involved in collaboration, such as listening, negotiating, accepting the ideas of others, which are valuable in their own right.

Before asking children to cope with a group task, they will need to have experienced a range of situations in which they have been called upon to listen, to discuss, to think together, to argue, to explain their views, to question and probe others, to report back, to play games together, to negotiate, to make a valued contribution and to accept feedback. Many of these will have been in the context of whole class sessions.

The group task itself must be one in which collaboration can easily take place. It will be more successful if the children can engage in it with a high level of motivation. This points to a problem-solving task which is directly relevant to their commonsense world.

The choices about which children are included in a group and of the size of the group are critical. Some of the more successful groups are self-selected, but friendship groups sometimes fail because the children adopt habitual roles. Many children need to learn to work with a partner - a group of two or three work less well than groups of four, which can break down into two pairs. The choice of who works with whom is made easier if we allow ourselves to accept that children will be at different stages in their development as collaborators. Some groups will be able to work more independently of the teacher than others.

When children formulate their own purposes ("Let's make a newspaper") and plan their own activities, they understand what they have to do and can proceed with confidence. The teacher's skill is to support the group to a worthwhile outcome. The children will need to be clear about what they are setting out to achieve, with a sense of purpose, knowing what a successful outcome will look like, how much time they have, and what resources are available. The teacher may need to intervene, particularly when frustration develops, to review the process so far and to clarify the next stage, perhaps suggesting that the children break the task down into simpler steps. Where children have not worked in groups continuously from the nursery class, they may need a structure for planning which they deliberately follow. Such a structure could be posted on the wall or presented on a task card.

A common cause of breakdown is disagreement over who does what. Sometimes it will be necessary to assign roles, or at least to ask the children in the group who is doing what so that their particular responsiblilty has been confirmed. In the case of making a newspaper, the roles could equate to those of a real newspaper, such as editor or reporter. Negotiating their own roles is not a skill which can be assumed.

Once the activity moves from the planning to the making stage, it is important for momentum to be maintained. When children are working together for the first time, or are inexperienced in group work, the length of time for each working session may need to be relatively short. Regular reporting back to the teacher or to the rest of the class gives the group an opportunity to see how they are moving forward and to obtain feedback.

Once the task is completed, it is important that the group, possibly with the support of the class, reflect on what they have made, so that they can enjoy their achievement, learn from their mistakes and consider how the outcome has succeeded in media education terms. It is also important that the group reviews its success as a group so that the children can see ways in which they might work differently next time.

A particular kind of collaboration activity is drama. All kinds of possibilities present themselves in media education, such as simulating scenes or advertisements, sketches, preparing video sequences, or freezing an activity to make a "live photograph". Many of the skills children develop in drama are applicable in group tasks and in discussion.

A difficulty of collaborative group work lies in the intention to hand over more control to the children. This involves risk on our part. The risk will pay off if we prepare carefully, establish clear procedures and expectations, and take care not to pull the carpet from under ourselves or the children too suddenly. We can only take one tentative step at a time.

6 year olds at Copplestone School, Devon, sequencing photographs to make a story. Photo: Sandra Sutton

Discussion

The value of discussion lies in moving children further in their thinking than they would move on their own. It is "collaborative talk". It is at the struggle points, when there are conflicting perceptions and children are forced beyond the glib to the threshold of their ability to articulate and of new thought, that the real rewards of discussion come. The teacher needs to model the active listening which is at the core of discussion skills. Clarifying, probing, questioning for more detail and eye contact are all part of this.

In a discussion, be it with the whole class, or with a group (which is easier), the teacher needs to keep questions as open as possible; if there is only a one word answer, or if it is clear that the teacher is thinking of a "right" answer, the thoughts are reduced. Our interventions should serve to widen the children's understanding, not to narrow it; to release potential as well as to control the flow of talk.

Indeed, the teacher needs to find ways of discouraging the children from using him or her as the focus of their comments. Sitting in a circle can help to achieve this, as can the use of an object, like the conch in *Lord of the Flies,* so that only the child holding the object can speak. Another strategy is to explain to children the idea of the chairperson who will direct who is to speak in response to raised hands (or, more comfortably, fingers). If the teacher acts as chairperson, but takes care to refrain from comments except in the form of summary, it becomes possible to keep the flow of the discussion with the children.

As with collaboration, it is important to recognise that children will be at different stages in developing their skills. Listening, keeping to the point, or seeing other children's points of view are skills which have to be learned and practised. If we recognise that the children are learning how to discuss, our expectations will be more realistic and we will feel comfortable about the control we need to exercise.

A full discussion takes place when several children are involved in the same conversation. Describing it in this way indicates that the groundwork for success in discussion lies in the informal conversations, one-to-one and with small groups, which take place throughout the usual school day. If the expectations for active listening are modelled and children are encouraged to express themselves close to their "struggle points", then effective discussions will ensue.

Samia es el Hakam, Badram Zamir Hussain, Natalie Webster and Kamer Bashir playing house at Kettlebridge Nursery First School, Sheffield. Kamer imitates his father's behaviour in watching TV. Photo: Sue Van Noort

9   PROFILE COMPONENTS AND ASSESSMENT

The areas of knowledge and understanding that we have described, and the attainment targets we propose, will overlap substantially with those in other areas of the curriculum. This is particularly true of English, and we have described our view of the relationship between Media Education and English in section 7, Relation to the Rest of the Curriculum (pp 56 to 78); but it is also true of Science, Mathematics, Design and Technology. We anticipate that other curriculum areas will also be amenable to the integration of media education concepts and activities. It follows therefore that the Standard Assessment Tasks which are proposed for national assessment of children at 7 and 11 should give opportunities for the assessment of competence in media education.

In order to clarify and summarise what such competence would entail, we propose the following three Profile Components.

Understanding of Media Concepts

Under this heading are grouped the *conceptual* attainment targets concerned with the six areas of knowledge and understanding that we have identified (ie those beginning "understand that ...").

Media Production Ability

Here we group the *performance* attainment targets concerned with the same six areas (ie those beginning "be able to ...").

Knowledge about the Media and Society

This includes the *informational* elements of all the attainment targets, but particularly media agencies, audiences and representations (ie those beginning "know that ...").

These components are of equal importance and are closely inter-related. We believe that they can be related to the profile components of other subjects: for example, Media Production Ability relates to both Writing and Speaking in English. But it also seems important that media education should preserve its own integrity, as *English for Ages 5 to 11* has noted (14.4, p.61), so that children can be prepared for possible later study of the media as a separate option. We therefore envisage that, in the primary phase, media education attainment targets should, as far as possible, be integrated with those of other subjects. At the same time, we think that teachers should become aware of the areas of knowledge and understanding, attainment targets and profile components of media education, through pre-service and in-service training, so that they can appreciate and take advantage of what media education offers to the whole curriculum.

We also believe that an understanding of media education would in itself enhance the way Standard Assessment Tasks are devised and used. Recent HMI publications and the report of the Task Group on Assessment and Testing have acknowledged the significance of media products in the development of SATs.

Given the importance that can be attached to children's understanding of media products in the assessment process, and the broad applicability of such understandings across the curriculum, it may be appropriate for Working Parties to recognise that across the 7-11 age range, assessment procedures seem likely to draw on:

1   Children's ability to draw inferences from an image or a sequence of images, graphics or a combination of these.

2   Children's ability to draw inferences from a photograph, product package, video or other material and to represent their understanding in other media.

A closer inspection of these abilities suggests that they also involve:

a   Recognition of the level of realism employed

b   The ability to place a media artefact in an appropriate category (eg documentary, docu-drama or fiction or, in more detail, travelogue, expose, marketing device)

c   The ability to link categorisation appropriately with interpretation

d   The ability to understand the way a particular story or account is organised in media products and to relate this to a particular point of view

e   The ability to imagine who might have to produce the artefact, why, and for what audience

f   The capacity to reorganise information presented in one form for representation in another.

Further abilities might include an understanding of selection and editing, of narrative voice, of the different readings that may be made of a text, of the manipulation of time, of caricature and stereotyping, and of genre.

Such considerations suggest that in addition to those issues set out in 1 and 2, the following might also be recognised:

Children's ability to recognise that all media artefacts are partial representations and that this partiality can be related to particular points of view.

Assessment procedures which draw on identifiable instances of inference-making, re-telling and critical understanding as described above are doubly useful in that they not only provide markers of children's learning progress, but also promote it. We thus urge Subject Working Parties and the School Examinations and Assessment Council to recognise the importance of media education in assessment procedures.

The examples of tasks given in the report of the Task Group on Assessment and Testing (Appendix D), can easily be extended to include media education components. The task for 7 year olds could include:

MEDIA: Question asked: Why do we choose the clothes that we wear?
Estimate possible answers: warmth, fashion, colour, parental dictates, convenience, etc.
Make a survey of children's clothing choices; record and present the results in an appropriate form.

LANGUAGE/MEDIA: Tell the story of this experiment using writing, word processor, storyboard, video or audio tape.

The task for 11 year olds could include using media and media categories as criteria for classification (eg, of all the images in the room, which were produced here and which somewhere else? Who produced the latter and why are they here? Which are on paper and which on other substances? What materials are used to produce the image itself? - ink, chalk, paint, etc.)

The "What do people need to know" question can be extended to "How might they find out?" which will raise the issue of sources of information including advertising.

We note that in both of the assessment tasks there is little space for imaginative and creative work and we hope that this will be taken into account in the construction of SATs.

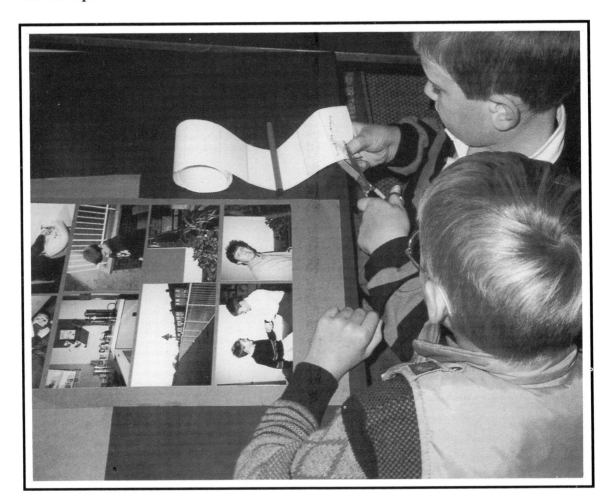

Adam Noble and Steven Breward, aged 8, making "speech bubbles" from sticky labels to add to a photo-story. Sherard School, Leics.
Photo: Paul Merrison

10 RESOURCES

The basic resources needed to begin teaching media education are present in all schools, for example, magazines, photographs and images in books and on display provide material for image analysis, and there are usually one or two single lens reflex (SLR) cameras and audio cassette tapes and a range of art and craft materials that will enable children to embark on elementary practical activities.

For media education to proceed properly and consistently, resources need to be dependable and organised methodically. It is desirable that an annual budget should be allocated to media education. This should be calculated to cover the costs of consumable materials: paper, glue, photocopying, still and/or cine film, video tapes, film or video hire. Small primary schools who are unable to finance the purchase of costly equipment should build up a thorough knowledge of what resources are available through their local teachers' centre or initial teacher training departments of their local polytechnic or univeristy, or through loans from feeder secondary or middle schools. Materials and equipment need to be securely stored, particularly if they are on loan, and yet easily accessible to teachers.

The following are recommended as minimal requirements which any school taking media education seriously should meet:

1   A classroom equipped with black-out facilities, moveable desks and chairs, display spaces on the walls, blackboard and screen

2   Lockable filing cabinets and suspension files where worksheets and slide sets can be kept

3   A good photocopier

4   SLR cameras (these are preferable because children can see the exact image they are making)

5   Audio cassette tape recorders

6   A television set.

Access to the following:

-    Reel-to-reel cassette recorder and splicing block
-    A video recorder with search and freeze-frame facilities. If it is a school resource, the TV and video could be mounted on a security trolley
-    A Super-8 cine camera with cable release
-    A Super-8 projector
-    A camcorder with rechargeable batteries

- An extension microphone
- Lights and extension cables.

Organisation

Since it is likely that more than one teacher will depend on the above resources, it is useful to have a simple, clearly defined booking system. How the school's media education curriculum is devised will have implications for timetabling and teacher development. Some schools use a media education specialist teaching modules on a "carousel" basis. Others devise courses for each year to be taught by all class teachers once they have had sufficient in-service training. The curriculum co-ordinator should be party to any media education planning, if only to ensure the consequences for rooms, teacher time and timetabling run smoothly.

Time and space should be set aside for the appreciation and evaluation of the media education work produced by children. Assemblies and displays should draw pupils' attention to their own and others' work. Evenings when parents can be invited to participate in media education work and discussion are also worthwhile and reward thoughtful organisation.

Child's photograph of boys, aged 6, processing a sun picture at Wombridge School, Shropshire

11 TRAINING IMPLICATIONS

If media education is to permeate much of the existing curriculum then it needs to be supported by a framework of pre-service and in-service training for all teachers. This will take a considerable time to develop, but will be an essential condition for establishing good media education practice.

Pre-service training

Ideally, all existing B.Ed and PGCE courses should contain an element of media education. The new teachers will face children who are steeped in the language and lore of television, video, film, books, computers and advertising, so it is essential their training prepares them for engaging with the media in an educationally valuable way.

In a small number of teacher training institutions media education already exists, usually as a component of Language and/or Literacy courses. With the recent publication of *English for Ages 5 to 11*, we hope that such components will be introduced into many more pre-service courses so that they begin to reflect the influence of the media in the child's linguistic environment. But in time other specialist areas such as History, Art and Science should also prepare teachers for media work in these subjects.

Another possible route for developing media education within colleges of education is to link it with cross-curricular areas such as Multi-Cultural Education, Special Needs, Health Education, Arts, Information Technology and Drama where there is a significant but often unwritten connection with work on the media. Child development courses within pre-service training offer another site for work on the media. These courses could examine the part the media play in the social, emotional, cognitive and aesthetic development of the child.

The form of media education course components will obviously vary according to their location. But in all cases, we would argue that student teachers need to grasp the basic principles of media education, and to understand how these are different from, as well as how they are connected to, the basic principles of their own subject area. This will entail some reading of media theory, if only at an introductory level, analysis of media texts, some consideration of existing teaching packs and approaches, and, where possible, some experience of media production. As a practical basis for these activities, students should be encouraged to articulate and reflect upon their experiences and tastes as media consumers; and to investigate children's media knowledge in the course of teaching practice.

B.Ed or PGCE courses involving a media education component are currently (1989) available at a number of institutions, including:

Institute of Education, University of London
West Glamorgan Institute of Higher Education
Trinity and All Saints College, Leeds
Bristol Polytechnic

University of Nottingham
University of Southampton
Christ Church College, Canterbury
Middlesex Polytechnic

BFI Education produces an annual listing of higher education courses which contain media studies elements.

In-service training

In most local authorities INSET provision has undergone recent radical change. There has been a movement towards school-based and school-focussed INSET. The National Priorities established by central government determine many of the INSET courses currently on offer in colleges of education. However, the school-based needs identification model which locates INSET within staff development plans, provides a space for those areas such as media education which do not appear on the list of national priorities.

How do teachers identify media education as an INSET need? At present, teachers who have a personal enthusiasm for media education, those who make contact with a local adviser, attend a regional or national conference or read about media work in relevant publications or often a combination of these, may identify work on the media as being important for their class and school. Other teachers may be concerned about the way children use television, and perceive media education as a means of defending them against the media. Some may regard media education as merely technical training, or as "common sense", ie something the children develop themselves. The identification of media education as an INSET need by teachers can derive from a broad range of motivational factors. INSET providers should be aware of this and construct courses, conferences, and one day events that will relate media education to good primary practice as: a cross-curricular theme; a topic permeating other curriculum areas, a single topic, or any combination of these three; helping to retain the breadth and balance in the curriculum.

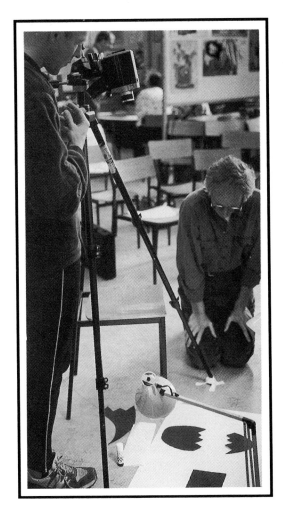

Teachers at the BFI Easter School trying out simple Super 8mm animation. Photo: Cary Bazalgette

But, as in pre-service education, teachers need to grasp the basic principles of media education and explore ways of relating it to their own practice. Where possible, extended INSET provision should relate to actual classroom practice, offering tasks for teachers to undertake in school, and opportunities to share and reflect upon these. Teachers should be encouraged to investigate and discuss both their own media experiences and those of the children they teach. In the early stages of development of primary media education, teachers can be encouraged to undertake and write up, or otherwise record, their own small-scale action research projects. It is usually after an initial stage of trying out media education ideas and topics, that practising teachers come to the stage of wishing to read and study some media theory and deepen their understanding of media education concepts.

In future, we hope that media education INSET will be given a higher profile. LEA Inspectors for INSET, INSET Co-ordinators and Staff Development Officers need to be targetted at their planning meetings to ensure media education carried on at a school or consortium level is supported and developed. BFI Education and a number of higher education institutions are beginning to develop distance learning courses for teachers in media education.

The citing of media education in the National Curriculum documentation and local authority Curriculum Policy documents could provide the necessary stimulus for school, teacher centre or college-based INSET.

Teachers already involved in media education work need to be given the opportunity to share their classroom experiences with colleagues at one day workshops or at longer residential courses. Many of the significant developments in media teaching have come from practising teachers in classroom situations. Word-of-mouth endorsement and encouragement of media education work by practising teachers is essential in maintaining support for education about the media. Wherever possible, teachers who have developed media work in their classroom, should be used as enablers for pre-service and INSET media courses.

The perennial problem of training is: Who trains the trainers? If media education is to become an essential element in all B.Ed, PGCE and INSET courses, those with responsibility for course construction need to be targeted as implementing agents. This might take place most effectively in staff development sessions or through the National Association of Teachers Educators and Advisers in Media Education (TEAME: University of London Institute of Education, 20 Bedford Way, London WC1H 0AL).

12 | RESEARCH IMPLICATIONS

Throughout this document we have stressed the provisional nature of our statements. It follows from this that much further work is needed to clarify our proposals and add detail to them. Many more classroom materials need to be produced, to support this work. Effective INSET programmes need to be devised. Many people throughout Britain are already contributing to these developments. From September 1989, BFI Education hopes to set up a national media education project in England and Wales, to broaden and continue the achievements of the Working Party. There is a need both for independent research, to monitor the impact of curricular changes and initiatives on a national scale, and for smaller scale qualitative research projects addressing specific questions raised in this report, for instance the question, raised in the Media Languages section, about the factors which influence children's understanding of media conventions.

There is also a need for classroom evaluation and we think that curriculum research and development can be effectively undertaken by classroom teachers, given time and, ideally, some INSET on research skills and methods. Indeed, such evaluation can also, we believe, be effectively undertaken by children (see No. 6 below).

As a starting point, we list the following areas for research and evaluation which seem to us of immediate concern:

1   Assessment of the appropriateness of the attainment targets for 7 and 11 year olds. Since these are completely new areas for assessment some evaluation would be helpful (a) before a programme of media education started, and (b) after it had been under way for a while. Also, comparisons between schools undertaking media education and schools not doing it would be helpful in establishing what 7 and 11 year olds can and cannot do, with and without media education.

2   Correlation between media competence and children's performance in other areas of the curriculum. What difference(s) does media education make to the ways children learn in maths, science, technology, art, etc?

3   Research into attitudes of teachers to these proposals. How are they working out? Are they understood easily, or with difficulty? Are they implemented easily or with difficulty? Is there opposition/hostility to this kind of work and if so, how does it originate? What motivates teachers who take it up enthusiastically?

4   What do children know when they come into school? This might be the kind of "research" teachers would want to conduct themselves. It might include information about:

-    media consumption (who gets a daily paper/comic, what is it, who has a video, who has been to the theatre/cinema/panto/concert; who owns a book (books) etc.

-    most watched/favourite programmes - a class survey

- assessing children's preliminary ideas of genre, eg by saying "how often is that programme on - every day, every week?" etc. Does it have actors, presenters, etc?

- assessing difficulties children might have with certain codes/conventions - confusions about real/not real, in the sense of fictional/non-fictional; time passing in real life as compared with time passing in half an hour of soap opera; whether stories can be "ended" if the resolution of the plot hasn't happened yet, even though the programme has ended, etc.

- assessing production competence - obviously writing, drawing, painting, etc, but also hands-on experience of keyboards, videos, cameras, etc.

5   From a pedagogical point of view, it would be important to use different techniques and classroom approaches for this kind of assessment, eg cutting out pictures from *TV Times* or newspapers and asking children to sort them into categories. The same could be done with magazines, eg stating differences between editorial pictures and advertisements. Stories can be reconstructed/integrated using toys or through "pretend" activites. It would be useful for the findings of this kind of assessment/research to be recorded, pooled and disseminated so a general picture could begin to be built up of what teachers can *broadly* expect of children when they come into school and of what gaps or problems there might be. Also children themselves can participate by observing differences in tastes and experiences between, eg boys/girls; older/younger; those with big brothers and sisters and those with younger, or with none; themselves vs. the grown-ups in their families; themselves and the teacher. (All this relates to media audiences and is pedagogical as well as research - but if it were recorded and shared it would provide a valuable baseline for future developments.)

6   Children can also learn research methods themselves. Media education can be used to teach very simple "sociology", "psychology", ie simple social science. This would involve learning about the usefulness of counting things; the *number of people* in particular categories of audience or fictional types; the *number of responses* people make to questions; who has the most to say about TV or books in the class. When an assumption is made, eg "Television makes children violent/naughty" or whatever, a useful response is: "How do you know? Which children did you ask? How many? Did they all agree?" Research, in the sense of putting assumptions to the test, is another critical tool. Knowledge about it should also enable children to deal more critically with "research conclusions" that are presented to them in the media, by asking pertinent questions and assessing the validity of the answers.

13 | USEFUL BOOKS AND MATERIALS

Very few teaching materials specifically for primary media education exist as yet, although publishers and broadcasters are showing an interest. There is quite a lot of "behind the scenes" type of material which can be useful for reference, but much of it promotes a professional mystique which runs counter to the critical approach of media education. Teachers will have to be prepared to select and adapt from what they can find.

FURTHER BACKGROUND READING

Popular Television and Schoolchildren (DES 1983).
The report of a group of teachers which sparked off a wide interest in teaching about television and a continuing HMI concern with this area. Reprinted in *TV and Schooling* edited by David Lusted and Philip Drummond (BFI 1985).

Television, Sex Roles and Children Kevin Durkin (Open University Press 1985).
Excellent account of "effects" research which explains why much of it is so dubious, relevant to arguments about violence, racism and gender stereotyping.

Taking Advantage of Media Laurene Krasny Brown (Routledge and Kegan Paul 1986).

Children and Television Bob Hodge and David Tripp (Polity Press 1986).
Difficult in parts, but the ideas in this book were a major influence on the Working Party.

Understanding Reading Frank Smith (Holt, Rinehart Winston 1971).
Smith's ideas about reading and literacy were also very influential on the Working Party's first approaches to media education.

Film and the Primary School Fiona Wright.
Free booklet from Film Education, 37-39 Oxford Street, London W1V 1RE; phone 01-434 9932. Film Education also produce free study booklets on some children's films from time to time.

TEACHING PACKS

Picture Stories Yvonne Davies (BFI Educatioin 1986).
Contains slides, printed photographs and extensive teachers' notes for a wide range of activities using and discussing photographs.

Starters Roy Twitchin and Julian Birkett (BFI Education 198??).
Written for secondary teachers, but could be adapted for use with juniors: slides and teaching notes for close study of television title sequences. Tape available for hire from BFI Film and Video Library.

Switch On   (Scholastic Publications Ltd, Westfield Road, Southam, Leamington Spa, Warwickshire CV33 0JH).

A 32-page colour booklet designed to make children aware of communication methods. The folder contains 32 photocopiable worksheets plus detailed teachers' notes. Middle to top juniors.

Junior Education November 1987 included a topic pack on media education. *Junior Projects*, no. 39, 1988, was on "News". Back numbers available from Scholastic.

Teaching Developing Issues Section I Perceptions (Development Education Project).

A teaching pack which offers strategies for approaching the topic of perceptions and images particularly with respect to the Third World. Intended for use in secondary schools, but some of the material could be used with top juniors. It is available from DEP, c/o Manchester Polytechnic, 801 Wilmslow Road, Didsbury, Manchester M20 8RG, or from Oxfam Publications, 274 Banbury Road, Oxford OX2 7DZ.

BROADCASTS AND VIDEO

Talk, Write ... and Read (Central).

Central have incorporated a programme on the media within two series in 1986/87.

Media Kids OK   Paul Merrison.

An introductory tape on media education, available with notes from the Leicestershire Centre for Educational Technology, Herrick Road, Leicester LE2 6DJ.

Teaching Media Matters   Sandra Sutton and Dave Stewart.

An introductory tape exploring primary school media education with teachers new to the subject and with parents. Available from The Media Centre, South Hill Park, Bracknell, Berks.

The BBC's coverage of media education has been uneven, in our opinion, but the *Zig Zag* programmes on Photography and Animation (first broadcast in autumn 1986) are very useful.

HOW TO ...... BOOKS

There are many of these and all are usable to some extent. We note here just a few that are particularly worth attention.

Animation

Animation Guide   Roger Noake, Macdonald Orbis.
Animation Stand   Zoran Perisic, Focal Press Media Manuals, 1976.

Photography

The Working Camera: The World's First Pop Up Guide to Photography   John Hedgecoe and Ron Van der Meer,   Angus and Robertson.
Taking Photos   Lu Jeffrey, Piccolo.

Video

The video cameras and camcorders used in schools are all designed for informal domestic use and do not demand any special skills beyond following the instruction book. The best way of learning about video is through practice, either using the camera on one's own, or through attending locally-run video workshops or courses. Neither of the following deals with primary schools, but they contain some useful ideas. Both deal with older age groups but are adaptable.

Video with Young People Tony Dowmunt, Interaction Handbooks, Cassell, 1987.
Television Studies Sue & Wink Hackman, Hodder and Stoughton, 1988.

Sound Tape

There is virtually nothing on this area that we know of that is of direct help to primary teachers. The following is useful and should still be available.

The Responsive Chord Tony Schwartz, Anchor/Doubleday, 1973.

General

A very useful book covering all areas, which may be tracked down in libraries:

Doing the Media ed. Kit Laybourne and Paul Cianciolo, McGraw Hill, 1978.
Practical advice on photography, super 8mm film, sound tape.

ORGANISATIONS AND NETWORKS SUPPORTING MEDIA EDUCATION

Education Department
British Film Institute
21 Stephen Street
London W1P 1PL
01-255 1444

Runs annual residential in-service course at Easter; publishes materials; offers advice on media education. *Visits by appointment only.*

National Association of Teacher Educators and Advisers in Media Education (TEAME)
Institute of Education
University of London
20 Bedford Way
London
WC1H 0AL
01-636 1500

Both of the above are sources of information about regional provision for media education advice and support. The BFI has co-funded advisory and teacher training posts in a number of regional locations; in addition, many LEA advisors (usually English and/or Drama) have media education as part of their brief. After the publication of *Popular TV and Schoolchildren,* regional working groups were set up in ten English regions. Information, materials and advice on media education in Wales and Scotland can be obtained from:

Media Education Centre
5, Llandaff Road
Canton
Cardiff
CF1 9NF
0222 396 288

Media Studies Unit
Clwyd Centre for Education Technology
County Civic Centre
Mold
Clwyd
CH7 1YA
0352 55105

Media Education Development Officer
Scottish Film Council
Dowanhill
74 Victoria Crescent Road
Glasgow
G12 9JN
041 334 9314

England now has two major media museums, whose education departments offer invaluable events, materials and training:

Museum of the Moving Image
South Bank Centre
London
SE1 8XT
01-255 1444
01-401 2636 (24 hour recorded information)

National Museum of Photography, Film & Television
Princes View
Bradford
W. Yorkshire
BD7 0TR
0274 725 347

14 | ACKNOWLEDGEMENTS

This curriculum statement is the result of dedicated, unpaid work by the following members of the National Working Party over the period 1986 - 1989.

Beverly Anderson	Teacher, broadcaster and lecturer in Education at Oxford Polytechnic (resigned autumn 1986)
Chrisi Bailey	Primary teacher; photographer; research fellow to the Ilford Research Project on photography in education (died summer 1986)
Fiona Collins	Advisory teacher in Educational Technology Advisory Team, ILEA; primary teacher; specialist in multicultural education (co-opted autumnm 1986).
Julie Cox	Teacher adviser for Media Education, Media Education Centre, Wigan; seconday school history teacher.
Yvonne Davies	Advisory teacher for Media Education, Shropshire; primary teacher.
David Duffey	Head teacher of Paston Ridings Junior School, Peterborough.
Richard Eke	Senior lecturer in education, Bristol Polytechnic; previously primary adviser, ILEA and primary teacher.
Ken Fox	Senior lecturer in Primary Media Education, Christchurch College, Canterbury (co-opted autumn 1986).
Avril Harpley	Advisory teacher, Northants Rural Schools Project; infant teacher.
Peter Hart	Primary teacher, ILEA (co-opted autumn 1986; resigned summer 1988).
Anne Hawes	Primary teacher, ILEA.
Anne Hennessey	Head teacher of Miles Coverdale School, London (resigned summer 1988).
Helen Kirby	Primary teacher, Newcastle.
Mary Lewis	Senior lecturer in Education, University of Sussex.

Yvonne Madley	Primary teacher, ILEA.
Vincent McGrath	Sony/ILEA research fellow on video in Primary Media Education; media resources officer, ILEA (resigned summer 1987).
Paul Merrison	Advisory teacher for Media Education, Leciester 1983-84; primary teacher in Melton Mowbray.
Ben Moore	Teacher adviser for Media Education, Newcastle.
Graham Sellors	Schools TV producer, Central Television, Birmingham (co-opted autumn 1987).
Sandra Sutton	Head teacher at Copplestone Primary School, Crediton, Devon.
Sue Van Noort	Nursery teacher, Sheffield.
Sarah Webb	Primary teacher, Hampshire (resigned summer 1986).
Tana Wollen	Education Officer, British Film Institute.
Fiona Wright	Primary teacher, Essex (co-opted 1987).

Cary Bazalgette convened and adminstered the Working Party from BFI Education.

David Green, James Learmonth, Elisabeth Matthews and **Mollie Sayer** made invaluable contributions as HMI observers.

Thanks also to **Dr Máire Messenger Davies** who joined our last seminar, and who contributed the Research Implications section.

PRIMARY MEDIA EDUCATION: A Curriculum Statement

RESPONSE FORM

We would like to receive as many comments as possible about this statement. Your response can of course take any form you wish, but we offer the following headings to indicate what we would particularly like to know. It is not necessary to give your personal details if you would prefer not to.

NAME:

ADDRESS:

OCCUPATIONAL DETAILS (place of work, role, specialisms etc.)

DO YOU TEACH ABOUT THE MEDIA?

IF SO, WHAT BOOKS/MATERIALS HAVE YOU USED?

HOW DID YOU HEAR ABOUT THIS CURRICULUM STATEMENT?

OVERALL, DID YOU FIND THIS STATEMENT: EASY TO READ AND UNDERSTAND/ MODERATELY DIFFICULT / DIFFICULT IN PARTS / HEAVY GOING / CONFUSING / TOO LONG / CHALLENGING / IRRELEVANT / HELPFUL / JUST PLAIN WRONG?

Where appropriate, please refer to:

- language used
- organisation of sections
- ideas
- examples given
- inclusions and exclusions
- layout and illustration

WHAT IS YOUR REACTION TO OUR ATTEMPT TO FIT IN WITH NATIONAL CURRICULUM REQUIREMENTS (eg attainment targets, profile components)?

DO YOU: AGREE WITH / DISAGREE WITH / FAIL TO UNDERSTAND
(either in part, or entirely) our choice of the six areas of knowledge and understanding?

IF YOUR REACTIONS HAVE BEEN POSITIVE, IN WHAT WAYS (IF ANY) WILL THIS STATEMENT AFFECT YOUR FUTURE PRACTICE?

ANY ADDITIONS TO SECTION 13 (Books and Materials) WOULD BE WELCOME; ADD DETAILS HERE.

Many thanks for completing this form. Please return it to Cary Bazalgette, BFI Education, 21 Stephen Street, London W1P 1PL, and mark the envelope CURRICULUM RESPONSE. Your remarks will be treated as confidential, and no subsequent report will identify any respondents by name or place of work.